Frank, Or, Dialogues Between A Father And Son [microform] : On The Subjects Of Agriculture, Husbandry, And Rural Affairs

Pedder, James, 1775-1859

FRANK;

OR,

DIALOGUES

BETWEEN A FATHER AND SON,

ON THE SUBJECTS OF

AGRICULTURE, HUSBANDRY,

AND

RURAL AFFAIRS.

BY THE AUTHOR OF
"THE YELLOW SHOESTRINGS"

James Pedder

"Agriculture is the noblest of all employments, as well as the most favourable to morals   Let the soldier talk of honour and glory, I see more honour in covering the earth with grain and verdure, than with dead and mangled bodies , and more glory in providing food for its inhabitants, than in destroying them "

"Nothing is impossible to a willing mind "

PHILADELPHIA

KIMBER & SHARPLESS, No 50 NORTH FOURTH ST

1840.

Entered, according to the Act of Congress in the year 1840, by
JAMES PEDDER, in the Clerk's Office of the District Court for the
Eastern District of Pennsylvania

C Sherman & Co Printers,
19 St James Street

DEDICATION

To the junior members of that most useful class of
society, Agriculturists, these Dialogues,—the reminis-
cences of a long life, devoted to the pursuits of agriculture, husbandry, and rural affairs, and in which the
characters are real, not fictitious, for there is a Frank
and a Sister Susan, a Grabb and a Sykes, the circum
stances also having "a local habitation and a name,"
and the observations and reflections being the result of
much experience and investigation,—are dedicated, by
their very sincere and affectionate friend,

JAMES PEDDER

February 20th 1840

ADVERTISEMENT

THE following Dialogues were written for the 'Farmers' Cabinet,' a monthly periodical, devoted to " Agriculture, Horticulture, and Rural Affairs," published in Philadelphia

The idea had long been entertained, that a small publication on these subjects, in the way of dialogue, might be made generally interesting to the young, and especially to the junior members of " that most useful class of society,"—Agriculturists, and one, who was, perhaps, of all others, the most competent to judge of these matters—a well known publisher of juvenile books in London—was decidedly of that opinion He was the publisher of that little book, " The Yellow Shoestrings," which has long been familiar to the young, has run through many editions, and still enjoys their patronage, and many applications have been made to the writer, for another manuscript suitable to that *department* He remarked, " There are many writers of eminence who have undertaken to write books for children, but they have generally failed to interest them, their style being above the subjects upon which they have been engaged—but all children like to read ' *The Yellow Shoestrings* ' "

It is, however, but justice to say, the immediate

inducement to make the present attempt, may be traced to a very interesting paper at page 279 of the second volume of the "Farmers' Cabinet," entitled, "Receipt to make boys industrious and useful," where the sensible writer recommends, "that children be permitted to exert themselves, and be as useful as their circumstances will admit of, and that they be furnished with implements or tools, adapted to their age, strength, and capacity, and *be soothed with the language of encouragement to use them,* when they would be sure to grow up to man's estate without being chargeable with the crime of laziness, their bodily powers would be improved and invigorated, and they would display more mental developement than those with whom a contrary plan had been pursued They should be provided with small axes, shovels, forks, dungforks, rakes, spades, wheelbarrows, scythes, sickles, and in fact every necessary tool for the performance of every agricultural or horticultural operation, graduated in weight and size, so as to adapt them to the age and strength of their juvenile owner, and if those who make tools would prepare sets of the different kinds of the proper proportions for lads, and of the very best materials, so as really to be useful—not mere toys—they would meet with ready sale, and the expense to the purchaser would be small, when compared with the benefits to be derived from their use." And he concludes, " If this plan were carried out by an *intelligent father,* who would give himself the *exquisite pleasure* of conversing rationally with his young sons, about the reasons of the various plans and pro-

cesses of agriculture, and take some pains to make them understand the philosophy of his calling, he would rarely find them indolent, or dissatisfied with their business, and seldom would they discover a disposition to exchange so useful and honourable an occupation for the more precarious and hazardous business of mercantile life."

The above was responded to by the following communication, which might be considered the commencement of the dialogues

TO THE EDITOR OF "THE FARMERS' CABINET"

I was much pleased with the proposal of your correspondent, page 279 of the Cabinet, " That our children should be furnished with tools suited to their strength, made in all respects like those used by men, their size and weight only excepted—*not mere playthings."* It is a happy thought, and I hope that ere long we shall be supplied with such from the stores, as a regular matter of business

Allow me to remark, in passing, our farming implements are made too heavy and clumsy, that they might have a greater appearance of strength—this I have discovered to be an error My neighbour Kendall's tools were made so large and heavy, particularly the handles of his rakes, shovels, and forks, that it was difficult to grasp them, and I have known his men purposely to put them under the wheels of his wagons to break them At last he got one constructed of light materials, and then the men looked out for that, and took care that it did not get injured This convinced *him* of *his* error

Too little regard is paid to the children of farmers, they are generally considered an inferior class, destined to turn the soil, of which they are supposed to form a part, and to be beneath the care and attention bestowed upon those intended for the counting-house or workshop—but why should this be? All admit that the employment is the most independent, and favourable to reflection and observation, and the time is not far distant, when it will also be admitted that the scope which it offers for experiment and improvement, is not inferior to what are called the *professional labours*

I have long thought that there is room for a lad's book on this subject, which, if it were well *got up*, might become popular, and be of great utility to the *most useful class* of the rising generation It might consist of dialogues between a father and his son, on the subjects of agriculture, husbandry, and rural affairs, and if the boy be intelligent, and the father well instructed in his *profession*, which would be found to embrace much that is not considered as relating to farming in the abstract, I am convinced that the work might be read to profit by other than mere children One thing is pretty certain—in the hands of an acute lad of twelve years of age, accustomed to "follow in the field his daily toil," the father would not enjoy a sinecure And to follow up the idea, permit me to give you a sort of outline, in the shape of a preface to such a book, for your approval The title might be, " Frank, or Dialogues between a Father and Son, on the subjects of Agriculture, Husbandry, and Rural Affairs "

PREFACE

THE *Grove Farm* is situated on the great western road in the county of ———, Pa, and contains seventy-nine acres of land the fields lie on the declivity of a hill, and the soil is so varied, that the different inclosures present almost every gradation, from sand to clay, that might be found on estates of ten times its magnitude The present occupier's father was the tenant fifty years ago, and by dint of good management, the son contrives to pay three times the rent which was paid by his father at that period

The family consists of a wife, almost unequalled in every desirable qualification, a daughter, fourteen years of age the pattern of her mother, and of the same name a son, Francis, of the age of twelve, and an infant The father is a working farmer, and Frank has been his companion since the time he was able to follow him into the fields, this will account for some of the inquiries which he will be found to make, and which, but for this circumstance, might be considered premature and when it is known that the farm is situated in the vicinity of a town, from whence books and other means of instruction are easily obtained, and that our farmer had received a respectable education, and his wife is a superior woman for her sphere, it will not be wondered that their leisure is spent in instructive conversation, leading to examination into, and reflection upon, the phenomena with which persons of such occupations are peculiarly conversant, or that their children are superior in attainments to the generality of those of their rank in life

As the soil of the farm is various, so also are the crops that are cultivated thereupon; and from the circumstance of the fields forming as it were a belt around the ascent of the hill, they are in general of small dimensions, being in many instances divided by small streams of water, and *vallets*, and courses and ditches, made for the purpose of carrying off the superabundant moisture, which in many places rises to the surface, in consequence of meeting with beds of clay in the substratum, giving the opportunity of practising Elkington's mode of draining with complete success.

From the number of trees growing around the house, it has taken its present name. At the time of the entrance of the present occupier's father, there was not a tree upon the farm—the owner, finding him to be an intelligent man, presented him with fifty dollars with which to purchase trees, to plant at his discretion, and from this trifling circumstance it is that the estate has changed its name from " Rainwells" to that of " The Grove "

DIALOGUES, &c.

DIALOGUE I

ADVENTURES OF A BONE

Father Well, Frank, this is the first morning of a new year. We have risen in health and safety, with a prospect of happiness; and although the times are difficult still we trust that our daily labour will procure us daily food, and a farmer in the bosom of a happy family, should be the last man to despair. We look forward to the spring too, and shall then have two summers to one winter, you know. This is the season, of all others, the most suitable at which to form good resolutions; we have enjoyed the festivities of Christmas, and now for the thankfulness of a grateful heart. You are now of an age when you might be supposed capable of reflection, and as you will accompany me in my employments in the field, I wish you to procure a book, into which you can write, every evening, whatever has passed worthy of notice in the day, and as far as I am able, I shall take pleasure in answering any inquiries that you might be led to make

In our way to spend a pleasant hour with our friend Sykes this afternoon, we must call at the mill, to order bone manure for our spring and summer use, for, judging from all that I have seen and heard, nothing can be so profitable as that, for dressing our upper fields, we shall then be able to give to our lower lands a double portion of dung and compost, at far less labour and expense of carriage

Frank How much we have lately heard of bone manure! I long to witness the effects on our own fields, eight bushels per acre only, will save a mountain of labour in the cartage of manure, if it be nothing else

Father Within these few years, bones have become an article of great request for manure and, horrible as it must appear to us, it is said, the battle fields of Europe, and especially that of Waterloo, have been dug up, for the purpose of obtaining the human and animal bones which they contained, and which have been sent, by whole cargoes, to other countries, to be ground up for manure, *perhaps for other purposes*

Frank It is horrible only to think of!

Father They are crushed by means of large iron cylinders, set with strong iron teeth, which draw in, and crush in an instant, the bones of a horse's head, while the fire will fly from the teeth in a surprising manner You have heard of phosphorus, this is obtained from bones, and the teeth are *supposed* to yield a large proportion, so that this fire is *phosphorescent*

When bones are ground fine, they are used as

manure for turnips, a small quantity being drilled with the seed at the time of sowing, the effect is truly astonishing I have seen portions of the same field, left for the purpose, without this dressing of bone-dust, by the side of those which had obtained it, the turnips, on the undressed parts, were not larger than walnuts, while those on the dressed land were as large as your hat, and sold for twenty-five dollars an acre, to be fed on the land, the undressed turnips not being worth the trouble of feeding Upon poor, sandy hills, where, to drag up any other kind of manure would be worth more than the crop, bone-dust works wonders, by it, as good crops can be obtained, as in the valleys by the aid of farm-yard manure and the crops of all kinds feel the effects for many years after To prove that animal manures are more lasting in their effects than any other, I will relate a circumstance, which took place forty years ago, the truth of which you may rely upon A boy, while rolling a crop of barley on one of the hills in the Isle of Wight, (England,) unfortunately fell under the heavy roller, and was crushed flat, and although the body was immediately removed, a great quantity of the blood was left where the lad had fallen On this spot the crop grew to twice the height as that on any other part of the field, and was of a deep green colour, and to this day, the same spot, let the crop be what it might, is still discernible from its greener colour

Frank To how many uses bones are applied! I have heard that from them is extracted the spirit of hartshorn, which is in such general use as a medicine, and I have lately seen buttons made of bone, almost equal in appearance to ivory

Father   They are indeed! and I have sometimes thought, that the "life and adventures of a bone," might be *worked up* into a very interesting story for children, suppose now we try our hand at it in the way of outline   We will, if you please, take the history of that wonderful horse Eclipse   I should say I have seen a fore leg of that surprising animal, whose birth, parentage, and education, must have been peculiarly interesting, how that he remained for years unnoticed, and was sold, for a comparatively small sum, to a butcher, to whom Colonel Kelley gave one thousand guineas for one half share of him, and laid a very large bet, that he would distance every horse that he started with on that day—thirteen in number—and that *he absolutely did it,* and all that   And that, after a most wonderful career of success, at his death his bones fell into the hands of a bone-boiler, who extracted from them the fat for making soap, after which, he burnt part of them in an enclosed cylinder, and during the combustion, the black, stinking liquor which dropped from them, was carefully preserved, and being purified, part of it was enclosed in a gold locket, set round with diamonds, and presented to Queen Victoria, to be worn on her coronation day, as a most valuable perfume, while another part was sold to a baker, to be mixed up with his dough, to cause it to rise in the oven, as light as a sponge, but which, after performing that office, was arrested in its progress up the chimney in a state of vapour, as it might be termed, and was

again sublimed in a glass vessel, to be again used for the same purpose, *ad infinitum*   Part of the residuum, which remained in the cylinder, it being *ivory black,* was used for the refining of sugar, while the remainder was ground into an impalpable powder and was sold to Day and Martin to make their *indescribable* polishing blacking!   Another part of these bones was burnt in the open air, the ashes from which were nearly as white as flour, part of these were used for refining gold, the remainder being mixed with flour, by a baker, to impart to the bread a peculiarly delicate whiteness, and to cause it to become light in the baking, excellent too, in the making of *wedding cakes!*   Phosphorus was made from another portion of the bones, with which to prime the lucifer matches, while the leg bones were made into buttons, for decorating the hunting coat of that same Colonel Kelley, as well as ornaments for his hunting whip, portions of these also were baked in an oven, until they had acquired a fine deep-brown tint, when they were ground down in oil, and formed the very colour with which Sir Thomas Lawrence painted the portrait of the beautiful horse upon which the Duke of Wellington rode on the day of the battle of Waterloo!   And we will suppose that the hoofs of this wonderful creature were burnt in an iron pot, and being mixed with potash, a fire blue colour was formed from the residuum, called Prussian blue, with which the blue riband was painted, which decorates the portrait of that famous man, riding upon that famous horse, which was painted by that famous painter!

And, to crown all, the remainder of the bones of

this noble animal were ground up for manure, and were used for a purpose by no means inferior to any of those above mentioned, according to the spirit of our motto—" Agriculture is the noblest of all employments, as well as the most favourable to morals Let the soldier talk of *honour* and *glory* I see more *honour* in covering the earth with grain and verdure, than with dead and mangled bodies, and more *glory* in providing food for its inhabitants, than in destroying them "

DIALOGUE II

THE ISLAND OF JERSEY

Frank Father, I have been reading the history of the Island of Jersey, (England) That must be a beautiful spot, and if the observation be correct, that high rents make good farmers, they must be first rate, that's certain Twenty-five dollars an acre rent must make good managers too, their *husbandry* must be equal to their *agriculture*

Father I am glad to find that you have not forgotten the definition of the terms, agriculture and husbandry

Frank I should be sorry if I did not remember that, *agriculture is the art of raising crops—husbandry the art of preserving and expending them*

Father Very well, and now for some account of both, as they are practised in that *school of industry*,

as it might very properly be termed My observations are the result of five years' residence in that island, during which I had the happiness of enjoying friendly intercourse with many of its first agriculturists

Frank I find that many of their farms consist of a few acres only, and that they sometimes contain *one field* only ! How do they contrive to obtain the means of existence from so small a quantity of land ?

Father Generally speaking, by selling their produce and living upon the refuse They eat very little animal food, a standing dish with the poorer sort, being cabbage leaves cut small, and boiled in water, and when done enough, hog's lard is added, and it is then eaten with bread, made of barley and wheat flour All their farms are small, my first introduction was to the largest farmer in a whole parish, who occupied thirty-six acres of land only, he did not conceive that any man could possibly manage more, and when my friend told him that I had known farms of a thousand acres, he replied, " Oh, he mistakes ! he means a hundred " As you say, many of the farms consist of one field only, yet upon this, they contrive to raise almost all the different crops first a strip of wheat, another of barley, and another of oats, always one of parsnips and the English broad bean, mixed, then their indispensable potato crop, with beans planted at wide intervals, a strip of clover or hay, for their next year's wheat tilth and present keep of the cow, and sometimes a patch of lucerne, the yield from which is truly surprising, and of which we must speak some

2*

future day Their gardens yield them vegetables,
amongst which is the Jersey kale, which grows to
the height of eight or ten feet, and sometimes more,
throwing out broad leaves, which they strip during
the whole summer, and these are fed to the cow, to
the pigs, to the weaning calf, and to themselves,
indiscriminately the quantity of food which they
yield is truly astonishing, and it is peculiar to them,
to flourish about as well under the shade of trees, as
in the open field, a fortunate circumstance, as the
whole island may almost be considered one vast
apple orchard, from which an incredible quantity of
cider is made for exportation A great part of their
wheat is sold at the market, in measures called
cabots, which contain about half a bushel each, and
they have a very simple method of separating the
finest portion of the crop for this purpose, which is,
by taking every little sheaf, and giving it a few
strokes across a barrel, lying on its side, these
sheaves are then laid by, to be clean threshed by the
flail at some future time, and this is done by lamp-
light during the winter evenings! This inferior wheat,
mixed with barley, furnishes their own bread The
beans and oats are ground together, and fed to their
fating hogs, they are at first fed with parsnips in
their raw state, afterwards these are boiled and
mixed with bran, and then comes the finish of oats
and beans Their pork is generally sold at the
market, the head, feet, entrails, and laid being kept
for home consumption Their potatoes supply them
with a great portion of their food, as also the cow,
pigs, and poultry, but the chief part of this crop is

sold for exportation to the Brazils, as well as to
England, as they are noted for their excellence. But
what they most value themselves upon is, the management of the *milk cow* she is the darling of the
family, and no wonder, for upon her they seem to
depend for life and breath and all things, and if ever
the Jerseymen become idolators, they will assuredly
worship the *milk cow*

Frank I have heard that these little cows, which
are called Alderneys, are brought from Jersey, and
not from the island whose name they bear, and that
none are allowed to be exported without a printed
certificate, describing age and colour, by whom bred,
and to whom sold, and that all this is attested before
a magistrate, who signs the document

Father All this is true, and as I have in my possession one of these certificates, which I received as
guaranty for one amongst thirty-seven cows and
bulls which I purchased there for a farm in Wales,
you will have an opportunity to study it in its original language, French Here it is—

Elevé par le Vendeur

Isle de Jersey

Pardevant un des Magistrates de la ⎞
cour Royale de cette isle   ⎠

A comparu personellement M Jean Le Gros, de
la Paroisse de St Marie en cette isle, l'quel déclare
par serment, avoir vendei a M James Pedder, une

Jenisse de son cru, de couleur rouse et blanche, agee, d'un an

Jean Le Gros

Jure devant nous,
  ce 4 jour d Aou, 1823 }
    Ph Marett

By these means they have preserved the breed pure and unmixed, a matter of great consequence to them It is hardly credible what a great number of these cows are exported to England every year, where, if they are very handsome, they bring great prices. They are a most valuable breed for the dairy, and astonishing accounts of the produce of their butter, is well attested—two, in the neighbourhood of London, gave nineteen pounds of butter each per week! Every farmer, therefore, rears a heifer every year for the English market, and this system alone has been the means of raising a fortune to many a man in that place, where, if a man has more than he expends, he is accounted *rich*, and this is the proper acceptation of the term *riches*—not what a man *spends*, but what he *saves*.

Then agriculture too is excellent they never fallow, nor do they ever sow wheat but in the spring, and yet, while the average of this crop for Devonshire is sixteen bushels per acre only, and for the Isle of Wight twenty-one bushels, the average for Jersey is thirty-seven! Their average crop of potatoes is 29,077 lbs per acre, and of a quality superior to all others but this superiority in quantity

and quality is owing, first, to their excellent soil, and next to their system of spade labour, and after that, to the culture bestowed by their plough, which, although heavy and awkward in appearance, is remarkably well adapted to their fine deep soils Their chief wheat tilth is hay or clover-stubble, this is skim-ploughed late in the autumn, or during the winter, early in the spring it is well harrowed, and upon this is spread dung or compost, or the ashes of sea-weed, and it is then turned down by a very shallow furrow, the plough, on repassing, taking a deeper furrow from the bottom of the trench, and turning it on it—thus the land is, properly speaking, *trenched*, and upon this is sown wheat, three and a half bushels per acre—a very large quantity of seed, but as there is not time for it to tiller and spread, as winter wheat is expected to do, it is necessary to sow thickly I have no where seen crops of wheat so thick or free from blight, which I attribute to sowing on a highly manured seed bed, the crop coming up and growing so rapidly as to bid defiance to the ordinary cold blasts of spring, this, being *necessary to spring-sown wheat*, would be highly injurious to that sown at Michaelmas, as it would too much encourage its growth, making it, what is called by farmers, *winter proud* but with their management I have known the crop to ripen in little more than three months from the time of sowing, even with wheat of the common red and white species, while the kind known as the French *tres mais* (three months), the real *Triticum cestivum*, is often cut in that time In Jersey they never turn down whole surfaces, but skim-plough them, letting them lie for a time, well harrowing the sod, and turning it down, generally by a double furrow, but this would be impracticable by any but such ploughs as are long in the waist, and sufficiently heavy to form a resistance to so thick a furrow-slice

As they keep a large stock of cows and calves during the winter, it is necessary that they should have a plentiful supply of food for them, and their management for a full crop of turnips is somewhat remarkable, immediately on carrying their first crop of clover, they skim-plough the land, harrow the sod, dress it with compost or sea-weed, and turn it, as above described, sowing turnip-seed broad cast, and I have never witnessed finer crops, they are partial to the tankard species, which grow to an amazing size Thus, in exchange for a precarious second crop of clover, they secure a mountain of roots for the support of their cattle during winter, and the land is in the finest order for a spring crop of wheat, which is often seeded with grass

Frank The large quantities of sea-weed, or vraik, as the history calls it, must add amazingly to their stock of manure, without adding at all to their stock of weeds—a lamentable evil where much stable and barn-yard manure is used—I should suppose they would also be lasting in their effects

Father The sea-vraik, as well as the ashes from it, are in universal request, but their effects are very soon exhausted the sea-weed in one year There are, however, inexhaustible supplies, not a storm arises but the shores are covered with them, rolled

into heaps, in some places larger than their carts A great many families residing on the coasts, obtain a living merely by drying and burning these weeds for their ashes, which they exchange with the farmers for wheat and barley but the chief supply is obtained from the rocks, with which the island is entirely surrounded, these are not permitted to be cut oftener than twice in the year, in the spring and summer, the precise time being declared publicly in open court, and then the period is limited to a few days only, during which time, however, all is hurry and bustle—every horse and cart is put into requisition, and thousands of persons, of all ages and both sexes, rush to the sea, and in a very short time, in the spring cutting, every meadow is covered with the black weeds, as well as a great portion of the arable land, and if rain falls immediately, they dissolve into a jellylike substance and wash away, if no rain falls, however, they dry up, and are then raked off, to be burnt for their ashes, in either case the effect is instantaneous, the grass grows remarkably quick, nor is it so liable to be affected by a season of drought, its quality too partakes of the nature of that from salt-marshes On their arable lands these weeds are immediately ploughed in by means of their fine plough, which turns the land *topsy-turvy*, and oats and barley and other crops are sown on a soil which, every morning for a long time after, is found reeking like a hotbed, occasioned by the fermentation of the sea-weed The autumn cutting is used chiefly as fuel for winter, being dried and stacked near the house for that purpose, the ashes are carefully preserved in some dry place for the wheat crop in the spring

Frank I have heard that meat, smoked with sea-weed, acquires a very peculiar flavour, very unlike that which is cured with the smoke from wood, and that it is much sooner cured, a few days being sufficient for the purpose.

Father It is true, and this difference might possibly arise from the circumstance, that the alkali produced from the burning of sea-weed, and all other marine plants, is *soda*, while that from wood and all land vegetables is *potash*, they also contain much animal matter, as well as marine salt, certain it is, the smoke which arises during their combustion, is much more pungent than that arising from the burning of wood Perhaps the Island of Jersey is one of the most fertile spots in Europe, its climate too is proverbially healthy, although it has the character of being very moist, many persons declaring that it rains three hundred days in the year these rains are, however, chiefly confined to the nights, the succeeding days being bright and sunny This circumstance has compelled them to adopt a peculiar mode of management in the saving of their crops, which it would be well to observe in other places, none of their grain is permitted to lie abroad after it is cut, even for a single night, it is carefully tied in sheaves, and is built up into small stacks in the field every evening, so much as has been cut during the day, and here it is permitted to remain until it is perfectly dry, when it is removed to the barn, they, however, adopt the same mode with their hay, which

is improper, for the removal of these stacks puts a stop to the fermentation of the hay, and is highly detrimental to its quality

Frank I have heard that in Jersey there are no taxes, that their own magistrates frame the laws, and that the government is independent of England, that it is, in fact, a little republic

Father In some respects it is so, much that relates to it is peculiarly interesting, and I shall feel pleasure in renewing the conversation at some future opportunity In the meanwhile, we must practise what we preach—we must "make hay while the sun shines"

DIALOGUE III

FALLOWING

Frank How is it, father, that you never fallow your land? All our neighbours fallow, and declare that it is necessary every four or five years, but why should it be more necessary for them than for you?

Father It is strange that the question of the necessity for fallowing still exists, particularly when the difference between the two systems of management is so great, amounting to a year's rent in four or five, and the loss of the produce of at least a fifth part of the arable land every year Some persons practise it for the purpose of cleaning the land, which, they affirm, cannot be done effectually without it, while others declare it is necessary, as a season of rest to the soil * Now, I have never yet found it necessary to resort to a whole year's fallow for either of these purposes, and yet I am sure that my land is more productive now, than it ever has been, and is much cleaner than the land of many of our neighbours who practise fallowing most rigorously But it is remarkable that many, who fallow for the purpose of clearing their land of weeds, will allow these to grow, and often to perfect their seeds on their fallows, between the times of ploughing! And this reminds me of a story relating to one of those who thus replenished his soil with a seven years' crop, according to the old adage, "one year's seeding is seven years' weeding" There was a sale in the neighbourhood, and he, being early, escaped a heavy shower of rain, just at its conclusion a farmer, an enemy to the fallowing system, came in on horseback, quite dry "How now!" cried the fallowist, "where hast been, to keep so dry?" "Why," replied the other, "just at the commencement of the storm, I was passing your fallow below, so I rode under one of your fine thistles, and sat, perfectly dry, until it was over, and then I came on" I have heard also of a favourite hog that had been lost for many days, and was at length discovered in a field that had received a whole year's fallow, to enable it to carry a crop of wheat, completely hidden by the weeds, which were growing and blossoming above its head!

Frank And now I think of it, no one ever finds it

* To the observation, land requires rest ' Yes," says an old farmer, "about as much as my kitchen table does after the men have dined"

necessary to fallow his garden, either for the purpose of cleaning or rest

Father That is an observation which I was about to make, and it is with me, conclusive, in fact, no one can *force* land to rest—it will continually be throwing up some crop or other, and is an artificial crop more exhausting than one of those called *natural?* unless, indeed, the countryman was right who, to the observation that weeds will grow, even in an unkindly season, replied, " Yes, but the earth is *own mother* to the weeds, while she is only *mother-in-law* to the crops that are planted in her bosom " Much allowance, I confess, must be made for soils, situations, and circumstances, it is to the system of fallowing, so religiously observed, that I object much also depends upon the ploughs that are used, many of these have the only quality of following the horses easily, but do *not cultivate* the soil, with such fallowing might be necessary

But I will read from my memorandum book, the management for the first course of crops on the new field, which I received from farmer Vincent in so foul a state as to be heart-breaking, as the neighbours termed it It was an oat stubble I ploughed it deep, and sowed it with rye on the 10th of October, the weeds sprang up, so as to cover the and like a carpet, but the crop was fed with sheep in the spring, so they had not time to come to maturity. As soon as the land was cleared by the sheep, it was ploughed, harrowed, and rolled, and the root-weeds were gathered and burnt upon the surface, it was then suffered to lie, and in a short time the seed-weeds had sprung up by tens of thousands; these were smothered at a blow, by being turned down by such a plough as the one which we now use; the land was again worked with the harrow and roller, and again were the weeds collected and burnt. In a few days another crop of weeds had made their appearance; they were again turned down, the land worked as before, and the root-weeds were again collected and burnt. This was the third cleaning. The seed-weeds again grew, but their number was exceedingly lessened by these operations. The field was then spread with soaper's ashes and stable dung, which were turned down by a shallow furrow, and turnips were sown on the 29th day of June on the finest seed-bed I ever witnessed. Thus this field had received five ploughings; the root-weeds had been gathered and burnt three times, and four plentiful crops of seed-weeds had been turned in and smothered, by the 29th day of June. The land was as clean as a garden—then why should it not be sown? Many of my neighbours, however, advised me to reserve it for a wheat crop, to be sown at Michaelmas. Another crop of weeds sprang up with the turnips, but these were destroyed by the hoe, and the turnips were the best in the country: the largest roots were drawn and housed for winter food, and the remainder were fed by sheep on the ground. By these means the land was so enriched, that the crop of barley which followed, was the best in the country, and the admiration of the neighbourhood; the yield was prodigious, and sold for an extra price for seed. Clover was sown with the barley, which after

harvest, afforded a considerable quantity of food for the cows; and during the winter, preparations were made for an early spring dressing of compost, of which lime formed a component part, and which, being laid on just at the first springing of the clover, caused a rapidity of growth, which brought the crop of hay to the scythe a week or ten days earlier than the generality of the crops in the neighbourhood, which was of great advantage to the second crop; both cuttings were fine, and the yield enormous. After the crops of hay were carried, a very large growth of aftermath took place, which was fed by cattle and sheep; the land was then skim-ploughed, the surface well harrowed, and turned down by a deep furrow, and wheat was sown on the 12th day of October. This crop averaged forty bushels per acre, and was so fine a sample that it was bought for seed, by those very people who had declared that "such management would never do in these parts." The instant the wheat was carried, the land was ploughed, and buckwheat was sown, which, as the season was remarkably propitious, yielded a heavy crop.

Frank. I suppose this mode of management ought to be termed *the new system*—I am sure it is in opposition to the old, which is in general use around us, and goes upon the principle of the new husbandry, *stint not, spare not.*

Father. That is exactly the state of the case. The old system was, to prevent the weeds from growing; those who practised it were therefore careful not to pulverise their soils, as the operation was sure to send up millions of weeds, which were afterwards to be eradicated only by a whole year's fallow the new system is, to induce them to grow, and if I can do that, I can easily destroy them at a blow, by turning them in with the plough My plan is, when I have no crop on the ground, to plough and harrow for weeds, and I am generally pretty successful in obtaining good crops of them

But we, who are of this new school, must be careful to *let our light shine*—we will therefore go and turn down those weeds which have sprung up in the four acre field since it was last ploughed That field is, as you know, designed for turnips, and no time must be lost in exposing, as often as possible, a fresh surface to the action of the sun and air; this is of equal importance with the eradication of the weeds.

Frank But could not the land be made sufficiently fine for the reception of the seed, by ploughing and harrowing and rolling, in one-half the time

Father When land is crushed by the plough, harrow, and roller, it is an artificial pulverisation, and if rain falls immediately after the operation, it will be found that it has done but little for the purpose, it is therefore, a most deceptious practice to sow any crop requiring a pulverised soil, after once ploughing, for, although it might be, to appearance, all that could be desired in this respect, the particles of earth thus forcibly rent asunder, will immediately fall together, drawn by the power of attraction—which we will talk about some future day—so as to exclude the atmospheric air, and then, the external pressure will

be so great as to bind the soil, so as to render it totally unfit for a seed-bed for the crop This pulverisation is perfectly different from that which arises from the effects either of frosts or repeated exposure by constant stirrings of the soil, by the latter operation, the earth is turned up to be dried and contracted by the sun and air, and afterwards, when penetrated by rain, it expands and falls to pieces, somewhat after the manner of slaked lime A soil which is thus pulverised, remains light and porous, and will be found to retain a degree of moisture, even in the driest seasons, for, acting as a sponge, it absorbs the exhalations which rise from the subsoil, while a hard surface rends open, and permits them to pass off into the atmosphere at once It is to this *natural* kind of pulverisation that Jethro Tull attributes the fertility of the soil, and argues, that the only use of dung, is to bring it about by its expansive effects during fermentation

Frank We now find the value of our new plough, which our neighbours consider a long and heavy *concern*. How completely does its wide wing cut off the weeds, and its noble mould-plate tumble them to destruction! What a pity, that it is not more generally known I now see the meaning of the term, cultivating the soil by means of the plough, the earth falls to pieces after it is raised by it, so as scarcely to require harrowing, and the surface is left perfectly level, with not a weed unburied

Father It will require but little harrowing, that, however, as well as rolling, it must have, thus the seeds of weeds, which are at present bound up in the clods that remain will be liberated and encouraged to grow, and then, as I said, their destruction is inevitable

Frank How totally different, indeed, is this system to that which is practised by all our neighbours! You see that John Lambert is turning over his large clods in the barn-close for the third time, and I heard him say he should not break them, for the weeds were already destroyed by the heat of the sun, adding, " The more you crush the clods, and the finer you make the surface, the more weeds you will have '

Father That is exactly true—the sun has dried up the root-weeds contained in the clods, and they are, no doubt, destroyed but the seeds of millions of others with which they abound, only await a convenient opportunity to vegetate, and that will be afforded them the first rain which falls after the crop is sown, when they will spring up and grow away with it, leaving him no opportunity to eradicate them I ought, however, to observe, it is not proper to pulverise the soil to such a degree of fineness for wheat, as *that* requires a close and compact seed-bed but you must remark that I never fallow for wheat, only for root crops, which have all the dung and compost that I can afford, so that I never dung for wheat, but reserve as much as possible for those crops which provide food for cattle, always remarking, the heavier these are, the larger is the dunghill the next spring And here is another observation of much importance—according to my theory, the weeds will spring up in abundance on a finely pulverised soil—now if this they do on the wheat crop,

they grow with it, and have time to come to maturity and perfect their seeds , not so, however, on the root crops, from whence they are easily removed by the hoe and cultivator So, you see, that our system is different from our neighbours from the beginning to the ending, and answers the purpose of fallowing, whether that be practised for the purpose of *cleaning the land, or affording it a season of rest,* for Tull considers that all crops are meliorating, until they blossom and perfect their seeds

Frank Yes, and I now understand why our neighbours fallow every four or five years, and declare that it is necessary—as indeed for them it is— and also, why you do so much better than they, without it.

DIALOGUE IV

OBSERVATION AND REFLECTION

Frank Father, I have just met John Ross, who tells me his uncle has lost two of his most valuable sheep by the rot, and that he fears he shall lose many more from the same cause, is there not a danger that our sheep will catch the same distemper, for you know they sometimes mix with them upon the common I suppose that the disease is communicated in this manner, for many of our neighbours are complaining of the ravages of that cruel disorder, the clods that remain, will be liberated and encouraged to grow, and then, as I said, their destruction is inevitable

Frank How totally different, indeed, is this system to that which is practised by all our neighbours! You see that John Lambert is turning over his large clods in the barn-close for the third time, and I heard him say he should not break them, for the weeds were already destroyed by the heat of the sun, adding, " The more you crush the clods, and the finer you make the surface, the more weeds you will have "

Father That is exactly true—the sun has dried up the root-weeds contained in the clods, and they are, no doubt, destroyed, but the seeds of millions of others with which they abound, only await a convenient opportunity to vegetate, and that will be afforded them the first rain which falls after the crop is sown, when they will spring up and grow away with it, leaving him no opportunity to eradicate them   I ought, however, to observe, it is not proper to pulverise the soil to such a degree of fineness for wheat, as *that* requires a close and compact seed-bed   but you must remark that I never fallow for wheat, only for root crops, which have all the dung and compost that I can afford, so that I never dung for wheat, but reserve as much as possible for those crops which provide food for cattle, always remarking, the heavier these are, the larger is the dunghill the next spring   And here is another observation of much importance—according to my theory, the weeds will spring up in abundance on a finely pulverised soil—now if this they do on the wheat crop,

they grow with it, and have time to come to maturity and perfect their seeds, not so, however, on the root crops, from whence they are easily removed by the hoe and cultivator   So, you see, that our system is different from our neighbours from the beginning to the ending, and answers the purpose of fallowing, whether that be practised for the purpose of *cleaning the land, or affording it a season of rest,* for Tull considers that all crops are meliorating, until they blossom and perfect their seeds

Frank. Yes, and I now understand why our neighbours fallow every four or five years, and declare that it is necessary—as indeed for them it is—and also, why you do so much better than they, without it.

DIALOGUE IV

OBSERVATION AND REFLECTION

Frank Father, I have just met John Ross, who tells me his uncle has lost two of his most valuable sheep by the rot, and that he fears he shall lose many more from the same cause, is there not a danger that our sheep will catch the same distemper, for you know they sometimes mix with them upon the common   I suppose that the disease is communicated in this manner, for many of our neighbours are complaining of the ravages of that cruel disorder, and are separating their flocks, to prevent contagion have you ever suffered in this way?

Father. I have never lost a sheep by the rot, but I attribute my security from this scourge, to *observation and reflection*, for while I am, as much as any one, an enemy to what is called mere "book knowledge," it is not possible for a farmer to follow his business, without being incessantly called upon for theoretical, as well as practical observation and reflection, and this, to an intelligent man, is his greatest pleasure Well might the good man of old, "walk into his fields to *meditate at eventide*," this is the proper season for *reflection*, the early morn for *observation*

Frank What a beautiful distinction! I must note that down

Father The disorder called the rot is not contagious, but is generally caused by cold and watery food, taken into the stomach, where, instead of digesting, it becomes putrid, and engenders life, the liver of sheep which die in the rot, is full of small creatures called *flukes*, something like flat fishes, these perforate it like a honeycomb, causing the death of thousands But it is a curious fact, that ewes, when irrecoverably gone in the rot, do not die while suckling their lambs, when these are weaned, however, they die off by hundreds And this evil is oftentimes much augmented, by their lying in low and damp pastures, for it is discovered, that the air which surrounds them in such situations, is loaded with poisonous vapour, which, being heavier than pure atmospheric air, cannot rise into it, and thus become purified,

but remains near the surface, and is inhaled by the sheep, whose heads are low, while larger animals, whose heads are above the stratum of poison, will remain in health, in pastures which are destructive to sheep Do you understand how this is?

Frank Yes, perfectly, and it reminds me of what I was reading but yesterday, concerning a cavern in Italy, into which, if a dog enter, it is destruction to him, while a man feels no inconvenience whatever, as the poisonous air, by its heaviness, is confined to the bottom of the cavern, it is, from this circumstance, called "Grotto del Cano" And, look at our sheep at this moment! they are all lying on that little rising ground, as though they were perfectly acquainted with the subject upon which we are conversing, and feel, no doubt, the comfort of the situation

Father True, and what will strike you very forcibly, observe that knoll, or rising ground, the next foggy morning, and you will perceive that it is in a clear atmosphere, while all the lower parts of the same field, and the adjoining lands, appear as though they were covered with water, the whole being enveloped in fog and you will be able to mark exactly the height to which the bad air extends But, even at the present moment, this poisonous atmosphere is there, although it is now invisible the coolness of the mornings and evenings will, however render it perceptible This is one reason why I always commence folding the sheep at the highest part of the field, that they might have the higher ground to retire to for rest, and, hence another advantage arises, which some of our neighbours do not seem to comprehend, the higher parts of the field receive, as they should do, the greater proportion of the manure. But I am confident that much of my security from this disorder arises from the use of lime, which is a corrector of the acidity of the soil, in the first place, and, in the second, is destructive to the whole family of aquatic plants—which are known to engender the disease—replacing them with those grasses which are *indigenous*, or native to a limestone soil, *upon which sheep never rot.* You know too, that I am careful to drain all wet and springy parts of the fields and this is a labour which our adjoining neighbours do not covet, I also allow salt for the use of the sheep, which is placed in troughs under shelter an excellent practice, which would, I have no doubt, prevent the disease, under very many circumstances

But come, now the weather is fine, we must think of the garden, we must be gardeners as well as farmers, for much profit as well as pleasure is to be derived from a good garden well cultivated. I do not, however, approve of doing much at this early part of the year, although many are tempted by a few warm days, such as we have enjoyed of late, to sow their seeds, which had better be reserved, March being, in this part of the country, early enough for general crops. There is, however, just one sort of work, which is peculiarly suitable to the present early season, and which ought to be done before any crops are sown, *it is, catching the mice.* I have often been amused with those, who never think of setting traps for these vermin, until they sow their peas, when,

after scattering them by handsful into their very holes, they stick up one solitary pea, to entice them from such a bountiful feast! I always say, as my father said, "first catch your mice, and then sow your peas," and by setting plenty of traps—the drip traps are the best—at this season of scarcity, you will be sure to catch every mouse in the garden

The season for pruning fruit trees has, however, arrived, and that business must not be delayed, for if mild weather come, the sap will soon begin to rise

Frank. I have often heard of the rising and falling of the sap, but have never understood what it meant, I can see that it *rises*, but does it *fall?* I ought not perhaps, to give an opinion, but it seems to me that the sap, when it rises, goes to form buds and leaves and flowers and fruit and branches, and is expended in these productions, and that, during the winter, a fresh supply is formed in the root, to be sent up and expended in the same way, the next spring and summer

Father. Older persons than you, have had the same ideas on the subject, the simplicity of the theory is inviting and sufficient for our present purpose, late researches have, however, given a different view of the interesting process, which will one day demand your examination and reflection. In the mean while, it is impossible not to admire the wisdom and beauty of the arrangement, by which "a new-created world springs up" at our feet, to gladden our hearts, and administer unspeakable delight to every sense, at every returning season of spring. You shall now see me prune this peach tree. I consider the management of trees analogous, in a very striking degree, to the management of children, and never take a branch in my hand at the time of pruning, but a thought passes my mind, *to whom is this like?* and I am not often at a loss for its counterpart It is to the management and character of the tree, that I consider the character and conduct of the man applies, and this idea might embrace all the trees, from the gooseberry bush to the most delicate white nectarine that was ever trained against a south wall You are aware, that all trees are not pruned alike, some requiring much more than others, nor do they need the same aspect, yet some trees are unfortunate in this last respect, and I never see the fine apricot which is stuck into that shady corner in Farmer Vince's garden, without pitying it, and have we not known *persons*, of whom it might be said, their situations in life are unfavourable? It is charitable to suppose, that a portion of the wretchedness which we meet with in the world, arises from that source, still more, however, springs from a neglect of *pruning at the proper season* Now say, if you perceive any thing which strikes you as remarkable, while I am pruning

Frank Oh, father, you have cut off the finest branch of the tree! it is tall as I am, and thick as my thumb, you have, I think, spoiled the tree for the whole year! what a quantity of fruit must this fine branch have borne in the summer!

Father In that you are mistaken, this beautiful branch, like many a beautiful child, was preying upon the substance of its parent, and starving the other branches of the family, without the least sign

of yielding fruit, and I never visit the city, without meeting many such fine and useless branches parading the streets, and lounging about the public places of amusement, and cannot help thinking, if they had been *headed down* at the proper season, they would at this time have been useful as well as ornamental members of society, comforting and supporting their parents by sheltering them in the winter of their days, instead of shooting above them and out-topping the tree, where they can be of no use, either to themselves or others, exposed to every blast that blows! Now, have you known any young man whom you can liken to this branch, so tall and so straight?

Frank Yes, indeed I have, William D——, and oh! how very like! His mother doted on him, and thought his health would be injured by the restraints of school, he could scarcely read, therefore, when she purchased for him a commission in a cavalry regiment, how fine was his horse, and he himself was as beautiful as paint, as his fond mother declared She gratified his every wish, but we know what use he made of such indulgence, after impoverishing his brothers and sisters by extravagance, the last we heard of him was, that he had been dismissed the service for bad conduct, and was confined in a wretched prison for debt! this was the last of him, not of his poor mother she died of a broken heart

Father Excellent! you have been very successful in your first attempt at reading characters, and I would have you follow it up, you will find it a study of great delight and instruction

Frank   But, father, you seem to be particularly careful of that little branch which you have in your hand, it appears the exact reverse of that of which we have been speaking, it is crooked and cankered, and the top of it is dead, yet it is full of promised fruit, now to whom can we liken it I wonder? Oh! to poor John Timms, the deformed boy, who lives at the corner of the lane, and who supports his mother, now that his father is dead, by going of errands for almost all the people of the village, you know we have often said he does the work of a little horse! that's good

Father   It is indeed a very correct likeness, nothing could be better. But here is one more branch, who is this like, think you?

Frank   Let me consider. It is not very large or fine, it does not grow in a conspicuous part of the tree, but seems desirous of shelter and support, it is not remarkably vigorous, nor has it a great profusion of flowering buds, I perceive, however, that every flowering bud has a *leaf bud*, and from this circumstance I conclude, that if the season is favourable, every flower bud may be expected to produce fruit, and that every one will come to full maturity, and above all, you have not thought it necessary to prune it back. Oh, this is sister Susan!

Father   My good fellow! let but my hope be realized, and I shall one day find a correspondent branch on the other side of the tree, which will as truly resemble—*Frank*

Frank   I have heard that my grandfather was the best gardener in this part of the country, was it he that planned this delightful garden, that brought this little stream of water across the hill, and caused it to fall so gracefully over these rocks, into the basin below, and then to fill the pond in the centre, in which we see so many fishes playing about, who planted these willows that hang so beautifully over it, and placed the seats under them so judiciously, that by changing our situation, according to the position of the sun, we can always see to the bottom of the water?

Father   Yes, my boy, it was he who did all this, and every thing else which you see, it is to him that I am indebted for more than life, and I feel a holy reverence when I think of my father! But come this way, and I will show you what else he did, and what, by his instructions, I have been enabled to do, in fulfilment of his original ideas, for I have never deviated from the plan which he first laid down, and to this circumstance, I attribute the success which I have experienced. The whole of what is now the garden and orchard, was nothing but a wilderness at the time when my father entered upon this—*farm*, we call it now, then it had a different name—waste. It had a thick covering of bushes and briers, and appeared a chasm, which no one knew any thing about. My father observed it had a southern aspect, and that the declivities on its sides were not so precipitous as had been imagined. I was then just your age, and as you are now *mine*, so was I then *his* companion. I remember the evening when

4*

he came to the determination to turn this den of brambles into a garden, and I shall never forget the ardour which I felt, on looking forward to the time, when I should see it as at this moment! He sketched the plan in an instant, and the next evening, the axe and the mattock were busily employed amongst the bushes "Now, George," said he, remember our text, "*nothing is impossible to a willing mind*," and I assure you we stuck to it, in fact, we surprised even ourselves In less than a month, the laborious part of the work was accomplished, and by digging down the sides of the glen, we were enabled partly to fill the centre, and in forming the walks, we obtained earth sufficient to cover the borders, which were elevated considerably by the operation, and thus were obtained these very pleasant terrace walks around the sides, so much admired by all who have seen them Still, however, there remained a hollow in the centre, partly covered with large stones, and to make what is called *a virtue of necessity*, he so contrived, that this should form a fish-pond, and he soon found a way to convey water to it from the opposite side of the hill, and by placing large rough stones at the top of the chasm, where the water first comes over the declivity, he obtained a waterfall of twenty-five feet, to this you approach from below, by a narrow winding path beside the pond, and it was his happy thought, to excavate a basin at its foot, to receive the falling water, and by the side of it to plant the willow, and place the seat, which is so much admired, as well as to plant the acclivity in such a way as, in summer, to form a retreat impene-

trable to the sun's rays You see that the walks in the garden are wide enough for persons to walk in company, this, at the time they were formed, was considered a waste of land my father knew better, for by having no paltry, narrow cross walks, he actually saved by the plan, which is now so much approved The four quarters of the garden, and the southern border are appropriated to the raising of vegetables and fruits, whilst the eastern and western borders are devoted to flowers, a love for which I inherit from my father and the care of these, being given to your dear mother and sister, I need only point to them, to show how well they perform their pleasing task The water which flows from the fish-pond, is made to fill the canal, the bottom of which, being covered with gravel, forms the water-cress bed, the produce from which is so superior to all in the neighbourhood, as to bring a higher price in the market, this superiority arises from the crop being grown on gravel, where it might be kept clean from weeds, and the water coming on, after depositing its filth and mud in the fish-pond above From this canal, the water is carried by a trench down the middle of the orchard, and then, either passes in a serpentine course across the meadow below, for the purpose of watering its surface, or is conveyed, in a straight course, down the ditch to the mill-stream, either way which is most proper

Frank As very much of the productiveness of a garden must depend on judicious cropping, would it not be easy for a person who is competent, to make a sketch, and give instructions upon paper on the subject, so that the owner might have at one view, the different departments under his eye, stocked with suitable crops · with directions when to sow and plant, how to manage the crop while growing, when to take it up, and how to preserve it, &c ? The course might vary, as on a farm, and thus be made doubly productive I have often seen two or three different crops growing at the same time, and in the same spot, in our garden, especially on the southern border, now this must be very advantageous

Father As I have often witnessed the inconvenience and loss of labour attendant upon a large garden on a farm, my object is, to have no more land devoted to this purpose than is sufficient for the supply of the family, my plan is, therefore, to make the most of what I have, and I can thus easily keep every part of it clean, and there is no pleasure in a garden that is not so But, as in farming, so in gardening, much depends on soil, situation, and circumstances, these must be understood, before a judicious plan can be adopted, after which, however, the thing is easy and pleasant I sow, at the same time, on the southern border, a mixture of radish, spinach, and lettuce , the radishes come fit to draw early, and this leaves room for the spinach to spread, which, as it becomes fit to cut, is cleared in intervals, in which dwarf French beans are planted , and when all the spinach is removed, cauliflower plants are set between the rows of beans, which, in their turn, give place to a crop of celery, which is planted in deep trenches, with plenty of dung , this trenching and dunging is peculiarly favourable to such another rotation of crops

the next spring I plant English beans wide enough to admit rows of late cabbages between them, these are planted after the beans have nearly attained their full growth , they are thus shaded by them during the hot weather, at the time of planting, and yet are not injured by being overgrown, for by the time the cabbages require more room, the beans are removed, and the land where they grew, being dug and dunged, the cabbages strike fresh root and flourish amazingly In the summer I plant, alternately, a row of Broccoli and a row of Savoy cabbages, after the crops of peas are removed , the Savoys are cut during the winter, and the space well dug and dunged, which gives an early start to the Broccoli in the spring, and insures large heads. I plant the land with potatoes, upon the surface of which I sow a few radishes, which come off by the time the potatoes want hoeing , and at the distance of about three or four feet, I plant English beans amongst the potatoes, these do not injure in the least the crop, and furnish me with plenty of the finest seed for next year's planting

Frank Our neighbours say, you are always fortunate with your early cabbages , few of them go to seed in the spring, nor are they so liable to blight as theirs, even when they plant from the same seed-bed as yourself , how is this to be accounted for ?

Father Very easily , I plant in the autumn, as they do, but never encourage the growth of the plants by moulding them up through the winter, *as they do* , to be sure they do not look so thrivingly as theirs during that season, but they are able to bear frosts and snow better, and in the spring, when their crops are giving promises which are never performed, mine are advancing surely, and amongst many hundreds, I have seldom any that go to seed By earthing up their plants, they render them more liable to the blight, which is caused by cold winds and frosts in the spring, for they have been reared more tenderly, just as little boys now-a-days, are more subject to take cold than formerly, when great coats were not so much in fashion

Frank But, now I think of it, you never mould up any of your crops, not even the potatoes

Father No, and to this circumstance, I attribute much of my success in gardening, and did you never remark, that I do not water the crops, even in very dry weather, while our neighbours are using the watering-pot almost incessantly?

Frank I have often wondered how it was, that our crops grow so well in very dry and hot weather without watering, but could not account for it

Father You have often heard the remark, " If you begin to water your crops, you must continue to do so " Now, I conceive, by watering the surface of the earth, the fibres of the roots of the plants are induced to turn upward in search of moisture, and are therefore in danger of perishing for want of it, unless the watering is continued, but if none is to be obtained from above, they strike downwards, and find sufficient to support them during the hottest season, provided the intervals between the rows are kept well pulverized by means of digging, the loose surface, as has already been observed, acting as a

sponge to absorb the moisture which arises from the subsoil, and to give it out to the roots as it is needed. And the practice of earthing up is, I conceive, improper, on somewhat the same principle, for the light earth which is drawn up around the stalk of the plant, induces the fibres of the roots to strike into it for nourishment, but when the weather becomes hot and dry, this soon evaporates, and they perish for want of moisture And this is not all the evil, for in drawing this light and pulverized earth from the intervals between the rows, many of the lateral roots of the plants are uncovered and destroyed, and others are left to perish, just at the time when the plant requires the most nutriment, to enable it to perfect its growth By digging the intervals, instead of hoeing them, I render unnecessary the watering as well as the earthing of the crops, and obtain advantages over those who do both, at much less trouble and labour

DIALOGUE V

DRAINING AND HAYMAKING

Father This is the proper season for watering the meadows, and I see that our neighbour Ticey is carrying abroad the dung on the fields above us, we must therefore prepare the water courses, and be ready for the first rain which falls For the reason which I gave you for not ploughing these upper fields

until the spring, namely, that they are so liable to be
injured by the wash of the winter rains, I consider
that what he is now doing had better be delayed, I
have often told him so, but he will not be advised,
although he perceives that I benefit as much by his
manure as he does, for as the drainage which passes
the foot of his meadow, enters our water courses on
the other side of the fence, and passes through their
whole extent, they receive the washings of the fields
above them, and I have sometimes, to convince him
of the fact, taken him to see the very large crops of
hay which we obtain by these means, but all will
not do, I shall now, therefore, open the courses,
and receive with thankfulness what he is pleased to
give me

Frank I have heard that the ground upon which
we now stand, was a swamp when you took it, how
did you work such wonders ?

Father It was indeed a swamp, a sheep could
not feed on it in the winter, and the grass which
grew during the summer, was worthless as food for
cattle After securing a lease on it for twenty-one
years, I commenced operations, by cutting a very
deep drain across the top, or highest part of the field,
knowing that *all the water must come from the higher
ground* The former tenant had gone to great
expense in underdraining in every direction, but
although the drains were well made and filled with
stones, they were useless, because they were not
carried deep enough to touch the clay, you know
that the cause of the water rising to, and overflowing
the surface, is, because it is obstructed by a sub-

stratum of clay, which it cannot penetrate When I
had cut to the depth of five feet, I almost despaired
of success, for the soil was still boggy and full of
water, another foot, however, brought us to the clay,
and immediately the water rose into the drain, and
ran a strong stream, until it fell into the course,
which takes it to the mill-stream below There were
then a few auger-holes bored along the bottom of
the drain, and all was complete This single cut
was sufficient to drain the whole field, but I ought to
say, it penetrates six inches into the clay at the
bottom, by which the water is prevented from overflowing on the lower side of the drain As soon as
the land was firm enough to bear it, I covered the
whole surface with lime, and in six months it was so
completely drained, and had become so firm, that
horses and cattle pastured it until Christmas I then
determined to bring the water back over the surface,
by cutting surface drains, and in conveying it by
them to the lower parts of the field, I have, as you
say, " worked wonders," for it is now the best meadow
in this part of the country I, however, attribute most
of the success of this part of the undertaking, to the
circumstance of laying the land dry before flooding,
and making proper provision for carrying *off* the
water as quickly as it can be brought *on*, a provision
which is often unattended to, in forming meadows of
this description To *Elkington* we are indebted for
the present simple and most efficacious system of
draining, for the discovery of which he obtained a
reward of one thousand pounds from the British par-
liament I say, *discovery*, for so it was, he had put

5

a man to drain a field, and passing him while at
work, on his way to the sheep-fold, with an iron bar
on his shoulder, and seeing that what he was doing
was, to appearance, labour in vain, he threw the bar
from his shoulder, which, on falling, penetrated the
bottom of the drain, and on pulling it out, the water
immediately poured through the hole! He had
tapped the spring as well as his ideas, which, like
the water, flowed out, and this was to him a source
of great wealth and honour I must get his book,
which is full of interesting plates, recording and describing this circumstance, as well as many other
instances of successful drainage in various parts of
the country I knew the chairman of the committee
of the House of Commons who voted him the reward,
his name was Colquhoun, he told me that Elkington
was a plain man of strong mind, but without education, and was compelled to employ others to carry on
his correspondence, and even the writing of his book

But I knew another instance of recovering a
swamp, still more curious, the herbage which grew
upon it was of the coarsest species, and the spot had
been noted for rotting all the sheep that had pastured
upon it for many years It was near a town, and
the experiment was made by the owner, a man of
large fortune, more for the sake of example to others,
than of benefit to himself, he regularly sent his cart
to the town during the winter, to collect the sheep's
horns at the slaughtering houses, these, he caused to
be stuck very thickly into the sod of the swamp,
which was so soft that it was only necessary to enter
their points, and they were soon out of sight You

must suppose it was a curious sight to see a field
stuck all over with sheep's horns! By the spring,
they had nearly all disappeared, and a heavy roller
passing over, did the business on those parts of the
field which were sufficiently firm to bear the operation The result was truly astonishing! a tenfold
crop, of most excellent quality, white clover abound-
ing This was many years ago, but I understand the
effects are still as great as ever no manure has since
been applied, nor does it appear that it will ever
again be required

Frank If this had been my field, I should have
named it Horn Meadow But I have always observed that the grass of our meadow is of a different
sort from that of Farmer Ticey's, and when both are
fed by cattle, it is plain that they find a difference in
the quality too, for while there are large patches of
his which the cattle will not touch, and where the
grass grows long and rank, the surface of ours is
eaten close, and no long fog is remaining on any
part of the field, at the time of removing the cattle in
the autumn, how is this accounted for?

Father The thick covering of lime, which I gave
it soon after draining, is the principal cause, but
since then I have often gone over it, adding more to
those parts where the grass was coarse, and where
the herbage was very short and fine, I have encouraged a stronger growth by spreading compost,
by which means I have obtained that uniformity of
crop which has attracted the notice of strangers,
while our neighbours pay but little regard to it,

although the quality of our hay, when compared with theirs, has often been acknowledged

Frank I have often observed, how much finer and sweeter our hay is than Farmer Ticey's, and when Robert Ticey has sometimes assisted me to fodder the cattle, he has observed it too, but neither he nor I can account for the difference in cutting our hay out of the stack, and that of his father's, ours is so hard and close, as almost to defy the knife, while to cut his, is a pleasure, and requires but little exertion, is that difference occasioned by the lime too ?

Father In a measure it is, as the herbage is so much finer and the juices so much richer But the greater difference is in the mode of making the hay Suppose now we try our hand at a theory of hay-making When the grass is cut, and partially dried and put into the stack, it very soon shows that the juices are beginning to ferment, internal heat is engendered, by which the air is rarefied and expanded, and escapes by the outer surface of the stack, this causes a vacuum in the centre of the stack, when, the external atmosphere being now heavier than the internal, the hay is pressed forcibly downwards to supply the place before occupied by the air, and this process goes on, so long as fermentation continues thus, the external air is prevented from re-entering, and the greater the degree of fermentation, the closer the hay is pressed together and its fragrant particles prevented from flying off and being dissipated Now, from an examination of this theory, how improper must be that mode of making hay, which is practised

in many places, where, after the grass is cut, it is left exposed to the action of the sun and wind, until its most nutritious particles are dissipated, and then it is put into temporary stacks, to be taken to pieces and removed to the hay-barn, just as the remaining juices are in a state of fermentation, when no further pressure can take place, and, in consequence, the damp air, having free ingress, the hay becomes in a short time dusty, and comparatively, almost worthless Where a large quantity of hay is to be stacked together, it should be dried rather more than is proper for a smaller quantity, but on no account ought it to be put together while in a damp state remember, that hay when put together damp, always becomes mouldy; but when too green, yet dry, it might heat too much, and too violently, but does not grow mouldy Hay, when properly made and not too long exposed abroad, will be found of a superior quality, it will retain more of its juices, rendered *vinous* by fermentation, and will be worth more than double the value of that which is kept abroad in the field, until it has more the appearance of straw than of hay

Frank I have heard, that when hay has been entirely spoiled by exposure to wet weather during the time of making, it has been completely restored, by sprinkling it with salt, while stacking

Father I have no idea that hay in such a state, can be *completely* restored by *any* means, this is too much to expect, for where a great portion of the juices have been destroyed, having run into what is called the *acetous* fermentation, how are they to be renewed? it is quite as much as ought to be expected, if the portion which still remains, can be called into activity, by the *septic* properties of the salt, you know that a small quantity of salt will produce and accelerate fermentation, while a larger quantity will prevent it altogether, acting then, as an *antiseptic*, and it might thus be the means of renovating the hay, to a certain extent, but not entirely

Frank. I have also heard, that hay is exceedingly enriched in its fattening properties, by being sprinkled with linseed oil at the time of stacking

Father Lord Egremont made a trial of the value of linseed oil for this purpose, and expresses himself satisfied with the result, and it is probable that it might be found of great benefit, when hay has been injured by the weather; he found it, however, of too heating a nature for horses and milk cows, but for fattening cattle and sheep, excellent, "coming out of the stack very moist and clammy" But I have never had occasion to practise either of the above receipts, for when the weather at the time of making is wet, I keep it as little exposed as necessary, and if I can bring it to the stack with the flowers, which are mingled with it, of their natural colour—that is my criterion—I am satisfied that nothing need be added to render it more palatable or more nutritious

Frank These lectures on draining and haymaking shall go into my journal, and if I continue to add to it as I have done of late, I shall soon have a book which will be worth preserving

Father Then just take one observation more, by way of a close to the lectures The best salt

for curing fish, was, some years ago, *made on a Sunday!*

Frank But you are not serious, no one can believe that for a moment

Father I do not wonder at your surprise, but I am indeed serious, and will, in an instant, convince you of the truth of the assertion It was customary, on the Sunday mornings, to fill up the condensing pans at the salt works with brine, and to damp the large fires, in order that slow evaporation might go on during the day, as the pans were unattended on Sunday; this slow evaporation gave time for the *magnesian* salt, with which the brine is highly impregnated, to deposit, and form in crystals at the bottom of the pan, it being characteristic of this salt, to crystallize at a much less density than *muriate of soda*, which is, you know, the proper name of our common table salt On Monday morning then, the brine, thus purified, and which still remained uncrystallized, was drawn off quite clear into another pan, where the evaporation was continued, to the crystallizing point, the crystals from this refined brine were large and pure, and were reserved, for the purpose of *curing fish*, and delicate meats From this *hint*, the process of salt-making has been changed, and the evaporation is now stopped at that point, at which the magnesian salt is deposited; after which, the purified brine is drawn off, to be crystallized in other pans, the magnesian salt is then cut out of these pans in a crystallized state, and when purified, it forms the basis of Epsom, Cheltenham, and the effervescing salts of the drug stores

Frank I am indeed surprised, but it is now at the simple and beautiful way in which such an improbable circumstance is brought about!

DIALOGUE VI

LUCERNE—JERSEY

Frank Father, you said you would tell me more about the Island of Jersey, since then, I have seen an account of the growth and produce of lucerne, a crop which you say, grows there, which is truly astonishing ! I find, that it yields four crops for hay during the summer, and after that, abundance of feed for cows and sheep Is it a species of meadow grass, or more like clover ?

Father It is much like a narrow-leaved clover, but the *blossom* is very unlike, being of a beautiful blue colour The growth and produce is, as you say, truly astonishing and having had repeated opportunity to make myself acquainted with the crop, in every stage of its growth from its cultivation, I am able to speak very decidedly to its great superiority over every other, provided the soil be suitable, and the culture well attended to The crops to which I allude, were so remarkably productive, and I had such constant access to them, that I was induced, every evening, to enter into a journal whatever had transpired during the day, worthy of

observation, but for this circumstance, it would be out of my power, at this distance of time, to speak so decidedly as to their rapid growth and large yield, I have now, however, an opportunity to quote *chapter and verse* from this journal, which I will do for your information

The Rev Mr P having a field of an acre and a quarter, which had been suffered to run to weeds and bushes, determined to clear it and seed it with lucerne, he had it, therefore, trenched with the spade, to the depth of the staple of the land, which was, in some places, very shallow, the substratum being a hard gravel By this operation, the richest part, or surface soil, was turned down on the gravel, and the subsoil was brought to the surface, to be enriched by future dressings The work was done for fifty cents per perch of twenty-two feet square, and the seed was sown broadcast, and harrowed in by hand On the appearance of the plants, they were not supposed thick enough to form a crop, but by careful management, the field has produced immense crops, both of green food and of hay The journal commences, 13th September Mr P 's field of lucerne, measuring one acre and a quarter, after soiling two horses and a cow during the whole of the summer, has already given three crops of hay, on that part of the field which has not been cut for soiling, to the estimated quantity of five tons The fourth crop now growing, measures two feet in height, although but three weeks have passed since the third crop was carried, and it will be fit for the scythe by the 20th day of the present month, a fifth crop on that part of the field which has been mown for soiling, is now a foot in height

21st September The fourth crop of lucerne, mown this day for hay

24th The hay carried in excellent condition, the weather having been dry and hot, the only preparation requisite was, to turn the crop once only, this crop is equal to any of the preceding cuttings

26th A portion of the field, from whence gravel had been dug and the part levelled, has always dried up, after producing one crop of hay in the summer, the substratum being impenetrable, that spot has this day been covered to the depth of five inches with fresh earth, preparatory to trenching and re-sowing

18th October The trenching of the gravelly spot has been delayed, but the shoots of lucerne have penetrated the earth through a space of five inches, and it is now determined to allow it to remain un-trenched

23d November A fifth crop will not come to sufficient maturity for hay, but there is excellent food for horses and cattle

8th April The gravelly spot is the best and earliest part of the field, scarcely an inch in space, without a vigorous shoot of lucerne

6th May Commenced mowing the crop of lucerne for soiling, a remarkably heavy crop, more than two feet in height

11th The first crop mown for hay this day, a

space six feet square, taken as a fair average of the field, yielded twenty-three pounds* in weight as soon as cut after one day's exposure, it had lost eight pounds in weight, showing that a gallon of water had evaporated in twenty-four hours, from this small quantity of green food

23d The hay carried in good condition, not injured by five rainy days, the crop lying light, by means of its large stalks, requiring only careful turning now and then

26th June. A second crop mown for hay, measuring two feet eight inches in height The weather has been remarkably hot and dry, the result has been, a growth in the crop, of two inches in height every twenty-four hours, the last four days

17th July The third crop of lucerne measures seventeen inches in height, the weather is extremely hot and dry, all the meadows are parched, and farmers are compelled to feed their cattle on hay, the lucerne grows away, as if it had a shower every night !

22d The crop on the gravelly spot has again failed, a first and second crop come earlier, and grow more vigorously on this part of the field than on any other, but after that, it suffers for want of a depth of soil, affording a familiar illustration of the parable of the sower, (Matthew xiii 5 and 6 verses) The seed which fell on the stony ground *immediately* sprang up, because it had not much depth of earth, and consequently soon felt the influence of the sun,

* Twelve tons, eight hundred and fifty four pounds per acre

but when the sun was in full vigour, it was parched, " and for lack of nourishment, withered away "

7th August　The third crop of lucerne mown this day for hay, a very heavy crop, many of the plants in blossom　From the first to the second mowing, one month and fifteen days, from the second to the third cutting, one month and eleven days, after this, the field was rented to a tenant, for thirty pounds sterling per annum

Field, No. 2

5th September　A piece of land was sown this day with lucerne seed of this summer's growth, unaccompanied with any crop

20th March　The lucerne, sown on the 5th of last September, with seed of that summer's growth, has stood the severity of the winter, and the crop measures six inches in height this day

4th May　Cut the first crop of lucerne this day, two feet in height

14th June. A second crop mown this day, equal to the first.

14th July　The third crop mown this day, twenty-six inches in height

24th August　The fourth crop mown this day, equal to any of the preceding.

5th September　It was on this day last year, that this crop was sown with seed of that summer's production the fifth crop from which measures a foot in height this day

Field, No 3

Major T sowed a field with lucerne, in May of last year, unaccompanied with any crop, three heavy cuttings were taken for soiling, during the summer, and on the 4th of May of the present year, it was mown for hay, a very heavy crop, thus, giving four crops, in the space of one year from the time of sowing the seed

Field, No 4

Colonel T has a field of lucerne of four acres in full vigour, the crop, after cutting, measured three feet seven inches in length, he mowed a third crop for hay from this field on the 21st of July

Field, No. 5

M A, Esq in breaking up an old unproductive meadow, for the purpose of seeding it with lucerne, adopted the following mode　In September, the land was ploughed to the full staple of the soil, and sown with winter tares, or vetches, these were cut for hay in May, and yielded three tons per acre　The land was immediately ploughed and repeatedly harrowed, and the weeds were collected and burnt, a plentiful crop of seed weeds soon made their appearance, which were ploughed down, the land was again harrowed, and the weeds were again collected and burnt, this was repeated, until the soil was as clean as a garden, when it had a very thick coat of well rotted stable dung, which was very carefully turned in, and lucerne seed was sown in September, without

6

any other crop , and during the next summer, it was cut five times, either for soiling or for hay   the fifth crop, for soiling, was commenced cutting on the 25th September

So far the journal, which needs no comment

Frank I have heard, that the Island of Jersey is very small, not more than forty miles in circumference, and about six miles only across from north to south , in fact not much larger in proportion than Captain Price's sloop's quarter-deck, of which he used to boast, being *three steps and overboard !* but if such crops as these can be obtained, the size is not of much importance

Father The island is very small, but it abounds in remarkable incident   It is a sort of republic, being governed by a chief magistrate, by the title of lieutenant-baillie, who is appointed by the crown of England, and twelve jurats or magistrates, chosen by the people from amongst themselves , the chief magistrate having only a single vote   A throne and canopy, are erected in the *Royal Court*, as it is called, on which the lieutenant-baillie is seated, and the twelve jurats, in scarlet robes, range six on each side, on an elevated platform   A military governor is appointed by the crown, who is commander of the forces, the island being a strong garrison , he has also a seat in the court, but no vote on any occasion, and to show his inferiority, he sits on the right hand of the lieutenant-baillie, on a throne somewhat less elevated   The court frames laws for the jurisdiction of the island, from whence there is only one appeal, and that is, to the *king or queen in council.*

There is perfect freedom from taxation, and every article, imported for the use of the inhabitants, is duty free , the duty remitted on tea, amounting to ninety-eight per cent , and on tobacco about *six hundred per cent. !* Foreign spirits, however, is charged, by common consent, with one shilling (25 cents,) per gallon on importation, as a duty, the sum which this brings, about six thousand pounds sterling per annum, is faithfully expended in repairing and improving the wharves and harbours of the island , the government being supported by fees of court   A custom there is, of charging all purchasers at auction, with two cents each lot that is sold, these are called *God's pence,* and they are religiously devoted to the relief of the poor, who are always foreigners , a Jerseyman would sooner die than accept relief in the shape of public charity

It has an admiralty, as well as a civil and a criminal court   All the estates in the island are entered and described in a sort of Doomsday Book, deposited in court, and are valued at so many quarters of wheat each, instead of pounds sterling, or dollars, this being the ancient Norman law in the time of Rollo, and if a person has an estate to dispose of, he takes the person, wishing to purchase, to the court, and introduces him as such , the proper officer then turns to the description of the estate in the book, and declares, whether there be any mortgage upon it, &c , and after the seller has fixed the price which the purchaser is to give, all the rest of the business is left to the court, who furnish title, receive the purchase money, and enter all proceedings in the *Book of Remembrance*, so there are no disputed titles

A strange law there is, if a son sees that his father, through age or infirmity is no longer capable of managing his affairs, he has the right to take him before the court for examination, and if he be found incapable, the court places what is termed a father over him, to take care of him   They tell of a young man, who complained before the court, that his father had lost his memory; that he could not remember *any thing*   "Not remember!" said his father, "I shall never *forget* the cruelty with which you have treated me!" and *they drove the son from their presence*   The criminal laws are very lenient, there is a saying, "a man must have strong friends to get hanged," a punishment which has scarcely been known to be inflicted for the last age, for forgery, the punishment is, the loss of an ear, and banishment —to England!   The post of public executioner is so odious, that no Jerseyman has ever been known to fill it; the office falls to the lot of some foreigner, perhaps a culprit himself, who is never permitted to associate with any one of respectable standing in society   The labours of his office are chiefly confined to whipping criminals, sentenced by the court, who are always from amongst foreigners, with which the island abounds, no fear of Jerseymen being found delinquent, they are proverbially sober, honest, and industrious, especially the women

A curious story is told of a former *Jack Ketch*, as the executioner is called, he was called upon, in the

way of his duty, to flog a housebreaker, who was tied to the whipping-post, all ready for action, when Jack said to the magistrate, "now I won't flog this fellow unless you'll give me a new suit of clothes," the magistrate refused, saying he had already received his yearly allowance of a new suit   "You won't?" said Jack, "then flog him yourself!" and threw down the whip! and the magistrate was compelled to comply, for no one could be found who would put the law into execution   This same Jack Ketch, with his wife, were afterwards detected in a burglary and were sentenced to be flogged, but as no one would condescend to do it, they were ordered to flog one another!   Jack began, and cut Mrs Ketch so severely, that she was not able to perform her share of the operation, they were then transported to France, but she took a dreadful revenge, for on that very night, she arose, and while her husband slept, she cut his throat!

But the most curious are the bankrupt laws.   It is necessary to premise, that by law, any creditor is at liberty, and as often as he chooses, to call his debtor before the court, and request to have him, and his books examined, to ascertain if he have enough property to pay his debts, and persons neglecting to do this, are sometimes placed in most singular circumstances, for supposing a man becomes unable to pay his debts, and declares his insolvency before the court, they immediately collect all the debts that are due to him, and summon his creditors to meet him at court, when the oldest *creditor* is asked, "Will you take all the property this man has (mentioning the sum,) and pay all he owes?" If he finds that the man owes more than he is worth, he, of course, declines, when immediately he is struck from the list of creditors, and can never more come against the bankrupt for payment of any part of his debt. Then, the next oldest creditor is asked the same question, and if, for the same cause, he also refuses, he is likewise struck off, and is for ever incapacitated from making any future demand for payment The next oldest creditor may find, that the bankrupt has now, more than the amount of his debts, and therefore consents, putting money into his own pocket by the transaction! On expressing my astonishment at the injustice of this law, I was answered, "It is not unjust, for these creditors were bound to examine the man's affairs, and to see if he were able to pay his debts, by neglecting to do so, they gave the other creditors reason to believe that all was safe, supposing that they, who had so long known and trusted him were satisfied of his solvency, they must therefore take the consequence, for they knew the law"

Many foreigners feel themselves much aggrieved by another law, which is sometimes enforced If any one rents a house of a Jerseyman, the rent to be paid quarterly, the landlord has a right, immediately, to cause an inventory of all his furniture, &c to be made, which he holds as security for the rent, which is not due until that day three months! and when the amount is paid, he may, that instant, have another inventory made, as security for the next quarter's rent, and during that time, the tenant must

not remove a single article from the premises, if he does, he is liable to be prosecuted for theft!

But the most unjust and unnatural law, is the right of *primogeniture*, (the right of the first born son,) which reigns here in all its horrors! The owner of landed property cannot "will" that it shall be shared, at his death, by all his children alike, even if he have accumulated it by means of his own individual exertions, but the law takes possession, and the court accords to the *first born son*, (not daughter,) the best house, and land sufficient to enable him to occupy it, if it consist of land, or any other property they might think fit, and when the daughters are called to receive the portions which the court has allotted them, the *eldest son* shares again with them, to the injury, and sometimes the impoverishment, of all the other children, male and female!

Frank Now that is scandalously unjust, and I would not live in such a country for the world, free as it is from taxes Is the island free from tithe, of the evils of which we hear so much in England?

Father There are tithes, but as the crops which are titheable are enumerated by name in their old law books, and as potatoes, turnips, and some other crops do not appear amongst them—for they were not known at that time—they are supposed to be free from tithe, how far the *letter* will be able to do away with the *spirit* of the law of tithe, I do not know The Episcopal clergyman of each parish has a right to demand from every inhabitant, a yearly sum, whether he come to church or not, but as that sum is only two and a half pence—five cents

—for which he is bound to furnish him with a seat at the church, there is no great harm in it, except on the principle of persecution, after this, all sects are tolerated

The women are the greatest knitters in the world, and you will scarcely meet one without the *needles*, within doors or without, even going to market with baskets with articles for sale, they contrive to carry it on, either by poising the basket on the head, or tying it round the body with a handkerchief, while those who enjoy the luxury of riding to market in the cart, knit all the way, and when they go collecting weeds from the sea, the *knitting goes too.* During the winter evenings, they have what they call *knitting schools*, at their own houses, and at the place appointed, the best room is fitted up for the occasion, the floor being strewed with rushes, and lighted with lamps hung from the ceiling, and here the girls come, and knit for life until ten o'clock, when the young men come, to accompany them home, and the girl who is most expert at the work, is pretty sure to get the first husband, it is said, that upon some occasions, a man's stocking has been begun and finished the same evening   Many of these girls have a singular *propensity*, which is, to spend every cent they can save—and they will work hard for it too—in the purchase of cloth, with which to make shirts for their *hoped-for husbands*, years before the time when they expect to meet with them, and some have been known to have, hoarded up against that time, many dozens of those *indispensables*, as a marriage portion to their intended lord, without regard to size or

length, so that, instead of cutting the garment according to their husbands, they must cut their husbands according to their shirts ! and I have known a servant girl, who, speaking of one of her young friends about to be married, remarked, " why she has but three dozen shirts in the world, and yet talk of marrying !" but these are the marriages that are sure to wear well, I never heard of a divorce or more than one separation, during the time I resided among them, and there too, they still religiously observe the beautiful ancient custom of breaking a coin or some article of gold or silver between them, when they betroth themselves, and it is said, there is not an instance upon record, where either party proved faithless to the sacred vow ! This reminds me of that beautiful song of Dibdin's, " *The Sailor* "

> " The broken gold, the braided hair,
> The tender motto, writ so fair,
> Upon his 'bacco box he spied,
> And spelt, for comfort, on the lid—
> *If you loves I, as I loves you,*
> *No pair so happy as we two* "

DIALOGUE VII

MANURING

Father This is the proper time to carry abroad the compost on the meadows which lie out of the reach of the watering system. Here is a short table, showing how many loads are required to cover an acre, the heaps being dropped at given distances

No of heaps to a load	1	2	3	4	5	6	7	8
At five yards distance	193	96	64	48	38	32	27	24
At five and a half yards distance	160	80	53	40	32	26	23	20
At six yards distance	134	67	44	33	26	22	19	16
At six and a half yards distance	114	57	38	28	22	19	16	14
At seven yards distance	98	49	32	24	19	16	14	12
At seven and a half yards distance	86	43	28	21	17	14	12	10
At eight yards distance	75	37	25	18	15	12	10	9

By this table, and a calculation which we can easily make, of the contents of the compost heap which we are now going to carry abroad, we may know, to a certainty, how far the heap will go, towards covering the whole of the field, a very desirable piece of information, for if we could not ascertain this beforehand, we might begin to cover too thickly, and not have sufficient to finish at the same rate, which would not, you know, be doing equal justice to the field Go, therefore, and bring the nine-foot rod, which you will find in its place, over the door in the tool-house This rod, you will perceive, is divided into foot lengths, and at the end of every three feet there is a *cross*, to denote a *yard* Now, if we measure the length and breadth and height of our compost heap, we shall find the contents in loads, in a very short time   count, therefore, as I measure, and put on paper, as we go

Frank. Just ten feet wide, three feet high, and ninety-three feet long

Father. We will first multiply the width of the heap by its height, which will give us the number of square feet of compost in each foot run, or in length, of the heap—

10 feet wide,
3 feet high,

—

30 square feet of compost in each foot run

Now, if we take the length of the heap, and multiply it by 30, which you see is the number of square feet in each run, we shall get the exact number of square feet of compost contained in the heap , and then, by dividing this number by 27, the number of square feet of earth contained in a load—or a square yard—we shall ascertain the number of loads contained in the heap thus,

$$93 \text{ feet long,}$$
$$30$$

$$27)2790(103$$
$$27$$

$$90$$
$$81$$

$$9$$

There one hundred and three loads, and nine square feet of compost over, and if we make six heaps of each load, and drop them at five yards' distance, we shall find, by the table, that, at this rate, one hundred and three loads of compost will cover three acres, and leave seven loads over And, as you know that this field measures three acres and a quarter, there will, you see, be about sufficient compost to cover the whole

Frank Well, this is a valuable table and interesting calculation "How pleasant it is to do things properly," as our friend *Sykes* says!

Father Yes, Sykes *knows* how very pleasant it is to do things properly, and the next pleasant thing is, to live in friendship and daily intercourse with such a man, on the scripture principle of action—" Iron sharpeneth iron, so doth the countenance of a man his friend "

Frank I believe that persons are divided in opinion, respecting the proper state in which stable manure should be carried on to the land, some say it should be applied in its fresh state, others advise that it be dried to a "pinch of snuff," who are right?

Father I believe, as in almost every other case, so in this, extremes are equally wide of the truth I do not consider, that stable manure in its fresh state, and before fermentation, is, properly, the food of plants, and to carry it abroad at that time is, I conceive, to deprive it of a great part of its energy, while, to dry it to a "pinch of snuff," is to dissipate a large portion of its bulk, as well as energy The best time for use is, after the first fermentation, there is still sufficient energy to cause a partial action in the soil, which communicates vigour to the seeds and plants, and they are, at the same time, supplied with a pabulum fit for their sustenance Perhaps, there might be somewhat of analogy between this kind of fermentation, and that which takes place on mixing sugar and water, this mixture, you have

heard, will produce spirit or alcohol on distillation, but *that* it will not do, until after fermentation, and when that has subsided, it soon turns to vinegar, so that, as I said, extremes are bad All animal and vegetable manures have a tendency to rise in the soil, this is owing to fermentation, which takes place in those substances, by which they are rendered *gaseous*, you see the steam or vapour, flying off the dunghill in the yard? that is, properly, *gas*, it follows then, that when manure is carried abroad in this state, it ought immediately to be turned in, but as that cannot be done on the meadows, the dressing intended for them, should undergo a more complete fermentation, indeed, I always prepare a compost, and find it more valuable for the purpose You know that *compost*, means *mixture*, this heap is *composed* of ditch and bank earth, stable yard dung, and lime, and having been properly *mixed* by turning, I value it equal to so much stable-yard manure You know there are several kinds of manures, animal, vegetable, and calcareous or mineral The first is, by far the strongest, and consists of flesh, blood, hair, wool, bones, &c ; and the dung obtained from slaughter-houses is, on that account, of three times the value of the best stable dung. The second is composed of peat, straw, leaves, and herbage of all kinds, and the last, of limestone, chalk, marl, shells, &c, all which will effervesce in acids and burn into lime

Frank But you have not enumerated the most common of all the manures—stable dung, what ought that to be called?

7

Father It has been called animo-vegetable, but come, let us go into the house, the dew falls, I see we shall have no rain to-night

Frank I have often heard you make that remark, but cannot conceive from whence you draw your conclusions

Father Common observations have generally some truth, and I often amuse myself by inquiring into their origin With regard to that on which we are speaking, I conceive that the cause arises from, what chemists call, *affinity*, that is, the desire which two bodies of the same nature and density, have to unite Now, during the day, the warmth of the sun draws up from the earth, a vast quantity of water, in the state of vapour, this ascends into the higher regions of the air, and remains in that state, so long as the upper atmosphere continues warm, that which rises during the night however, becomes condensed by the cold evening and night air, and falls back on the earth in drops of dew, or water but when the upper atmosphere becomes colder than the lower region, there is an inclination in the vapour contained in the upper atmosphere to condense, and then, the exhalations of the night arise through the warmer or lower region, for the purpose of meeting the falling shower —on the principle of affinity—and both descend together

Frank I wonder why farmers are generally accounted an uninformed class? it certainly is not for want of opportunity to exercise their mind and judgment, they are surrounded with wonders, and I begin to hope, that every thing will not be discovered

before I become a man, as I once feared would be the case

Father With many persons, agriculture is a subject which ought not to be reasoned upon, or inquired into, and this is, no doubt the cause, why farmers are generally considered the least cultivated class of society, but I see not why this should be—with *us*, it ought not to be Another observation is, that it is colder just before sunrise in the morning, than it has been during the night, even in the severest weather, and I have had opportunities of verifying the truth of the remark I was once folding sheep before sunrise in the month of January, it was sufficiently light for me to see the sheep as they were lying around me, and there was nothing remarkable to call my attention, in an instant, however, and just before the rising of the sun, they became covered with hoar frost! I thought of what I had so often heard, and was certain that I felt as well as saw, the truth of the observation

Frank And did you endeavour to account for, what I suppose it may be called, this phenomenon?

Father Yes I did, at the time it was before me At the rising of the sun, or more properly, just before that takes place with us, the upper region of the atmosphere becomes suddenly illuminated and warmed, which causes an immediate expansion there, the lower region is thus, as it were, pressed forcibly downwards, and becomes condensed into water or hoar frost, as the case might be, the effect of which is sensibly felt by all who happen to be exposed to it The remark has often been made by the night coachman, particularly by the driver of the Norwich mail into London, by the way of Hackney, who describes the latter part of the journey, about Cambridge Heath, as far colder than what is felt on any other part of the road, there he passes, in the cold and shortest days, before the time of sunrise. It is also said, that on every *calm* morning the wind blows towards the east at the time of sunrise, although it has blown before, and might again blow after, from some other point of the compass, this too I have observed, but never without emotion it appears a sort of devotion which Creation is paying to the rising sun, and on a fine spring morning, when accompanied by the voices of animated nature, the effect is indescribable. This is caused, I conceive, by the rarefaction of the upper region of the air, which creates, as it were, a vacuum, to which the surrounding atmosphere rushes, for the purpose of supplying, or filling, the void, the air drawing towards the sun—the east—as air draws towards the fire, but this phenomenon cannot, properly, be witnessed, until the sun has risen, so that the air is warmed by its rays, and at this moment might often be heard, what is generally considered a creation of the fancy—*the music of spheres*—so often spoken of in descriptive works, this rushing sound, fabulously supposed to proceed from the chariot wheels of the "car of Phœbus," I have often heard, and the same effect, arising from the same cause, namely, the rarefaction or expansion of air, when coming in contact with heat, might be noticed, while sitting around the fire on a cold quiet evening, when the rushing of the air towards the fire, causes a sound distinctly audible.

Frank. I shall never again see the sun rise, without feeling much more interest about it than I have hitherto done. I do not wonder that many of the heathen nations worship the sun, and especially at its rising! I am sure it is, in the absence of *Him who made the sun*, the first object worthy of their regard and adoration!

Father. There is one more observation which I wish to make. While in England, I had often heard it said, there is but little evening twilight in America, the day closing almost suddenly on the departure of the sun, and thus the inhabitants are deprived of the most pleasureable part of the day. Now this, it must be acknowledged, is the fact, and although I have never heard the circumstance accounted for, it must be occasioned by the different circumstances and situations of the two countries, in England, the great Atlantic ocean lies to the westward, the sun setting over it, its rays are refracted by the surface of the waters, and the air is illuminated, long after the sun has sunk below the horizon, while here, on the seaboard of America, the Atlantic ocean lies to the eastward, and the sun sets amidst the dense woods of the forest in the west, from whence no rays can be refracted. Now, if this our theory be correct, we ought to find the difference between the morning and evening twilight to be reversed—the morning twilight in America should be the longest.

Frank. And so, I am sure, it is! *that's fact.* Now I guess that is something new, and worth remembering.

Father. We shall find it necessary to take advan-

7*

tage of this circumstance for a few days to come, and take the top of the morning, for as we mean to plough up the four acre field while the weather is open and the land free from frost, and as the ridges of the field are very short, in consequence of its triangular shape, we shall find a sensible difference in the length of our days' work, these *lengthening*, in proportion to the *shortening* of the land

Frank But, father, is not an acre of land *an acre*, wherever it is ?

Father Yes, and although you must have noticed the difference of time requisite to turn an acre, when the land is long, compared with the time consumed in turnings, when the land is short, neither you or any one else could possibly believe the difference to be so great as it really is   Here is a table, showing that difference, and a most interesting one it is

PLOUGHING

NAMES OF FIELDS	Length of ridges	Breadth to give an acre	Breadth of the furrow slice	Number of furrows in an acre	Time that it takes in turning		Time spent in turning the soil		No. of hours in the day's work
	yards		inches		h	m	h	m	hours
Short Lands	78	186	8	279	4	39	3	21	8
Harper's Hill	149	98		147	2	27	5	33	
South Mills	200	73		109	1	49	6	11	
Eastbourne	212	69		103	1	43	6	17	
Long Croft	274	53		79	1	19	6	41	

When the ridges are no more than seventy-eight yards long, four hours and thirty-nine minutes are spent in *turnings*, in a journey of eight hours !—more than half the day—whereas, when the ridges are two hundred and seventy-four yards long, one hour and nineteen minutes are sufficient, in the same length of time

Frank Indeed, no one would have calculated the amazing difference, and the next time I hear of ploughing against time, I shall not fail to inquire, what was the length of the ridges

---

DIALOGUE VIII.

LIME.—PROPENSITY

Frank I observe, father, that in all your compost heaps you use large quantities of lime

Father Yes, I consider that mode of expending it, the best and most economical that can be adopted, as it is enabled to act in its fourfold capacity to the greatest advantage, first, as a corrector of acidity, second, as a *stimulant*, third, as a *sweetener*, according to the beautiful simile of the preacher, who observed, " lime, to a stubborn, sour soil, is like the grace of God to a wicked man's heart," and fourth, as a destroyer of all weeds, with their seeds, and all noxious insects, with their eggs and progeny.

First. Our compost heaps are *composed* chiefly of

the earth from the openings of ditches, the scrapings of roads, and large clods cut from the sides of the highways, and from the margins of rivers and woods, all which, if applied immediately, as a dressing to the soil, would be injurious, rather than otherwise, in consequence of the acidity which they contain, lime is a corrector of that evil

Second And the heat, which is engendered at the time of its slaking, adds exceedingly to its powers in this respect, expanding and dividing the hardest clods in a surprising manner, and breaking up and pulverising the most compact masses, in an incredibly short space of time, they, in then turn, imbibing, and preventing the vapour which arises, from flying off and being dissipated

Third And here, the effect is truly astonishing, that which was before stubborn, inert and unyielding, becomes mild and generous, what was before injurious to vegetation, fit for the support of the most delicate herbs and flowers, and rendering the soil with which it is mixed, light and friable, warmer in winter and cooler in summer

Frank Warmer in winter and cooler in summer!

Father Yes, the soil, made lighter, and consequently more porous by the action of the lime, permits the superabundance of moisture in winter to pass off, while its absorbent qualities retain the moisture in hot weather, and the whiteness of colour which it communicates to the soil, mitigates the power of the sun's rays, put your hand on this dark-coloured door, now the sun is shining on it

Frank Why, it is burning hot!

Father Now, place it on the door frame, which is painted white

Frank I declare it is quite cool!

Father The dark colour absorbs the rays of the sun, the white colour throws them off It is a pretty experiment, although a common one, to place two pieces of cloth, one black and the other white, on the snow when the sun is shining, the black cloth soon sinks into the snow, which is melted by the rays of the sun passing through it, the snow, under the white cloth, is not affected in the least

Frank Then, now I understand why you keep the outside of the dairy, even the shingles on the roof, so nicely whitewashed, it is, to throw off the rays of the sun, by which means the house is kept so cool, even in the hottest weather, as to draw the notice of every one who enters it

Father Just so, in short, lime, like leaven, "leaveneth the whole lump" And,

Fourth The violent degree of heat, evolved during the slaking, is destructive of the weeds and their seeds, of which these clods are full, the deposites and seeding of many years, as also to worms, slugs, bugs and other vermin, and insects, roasting *their eggs* and turning them into valuable manure But you must have observed, and I have been expecting that you would notice the circumstance, that I do not mix the manure with the lime and sods on the first fermentation of the heaps, but delay doing so, until the time of turning them

Frank I have observed that, and ought to have noticed it, but my head was so full of the idea of cooking the vermin and roasting their eggs, with the probability of furnishing a dish of roasted onions for the treat, that I let slip the proper opportunity, I should have remembered it presently, I know, but do tell me, why you delay mixing the dung with the lime and sods, until the time of turning the heap?

Father There are two reasons which weigh with me, and which I will mention First, I conceive, that the dung would be injured by the violent heat of the lime, and a great portion of the most valuable part of it would be driven off and lost, by its action while in process of slaking, and second, because I think it very probable that, should the dung come into contact with the lime, while in such large and unmixed masses, it might operate as an *antiseptic*, (you know the meaning of that term,) and prevent decomposition, rather than a *septic*, or agent of dissolution Our object is, you know, to dissolve or decompose the mass, so, when the violent heat and action of the lime has subsided, and the clods are well broken up and mixed, I then add the dung, which soon becomes so decomposed, as to form with it a pulverised compost, peculiarly fitted for top-dressing the meadows and young clovers, and bringing the crop to the scythe so early, as to leave time for a second crop of hay, or a crop of seed, to come to full maturity, wheat always following on the clover lay

Frank But it would be inconvenient to you to use so much lime if you did not burn it for yourself I have often thought that, if you would describe your very convenient lime-burning establishment, and publish the account in the "Farmer's Cabinet," it might

prove of great service to many, who are so situated as to be able to take the benefit of your experience.

Father This is very probable, suppose then, we describe our lime-kiln, and the situation in which it is placed, as also the mode of working it? as you say, some persons might be benefited by it, and this consideration ought to be an inducement to us to communicate what we know Our kiln then, is situated at the entrance of the wood, and adjoining the public road, from whence a way leads to the top of the kiln on a gradual ascent It is placed in a bank, which has been excavated to receive it, this facilitates the ascent, and by this road the lime-stones and fuel are conducted to the top, without much labour It is built of the common stones of the country, the largest being selected, and roughly dressed or squared for the purpose, the walls being two feet thick. It is egg-shaped, and the dimensions are—shall we make a drawing of it?

Frank O yes! pray do

Father Well, then, there it is—

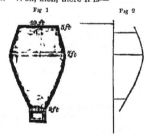

Fig 1   Fig 2

Ten feet deep, seven feet in diameter in the centre, five feet diameter at the top, two feet diameter at bottom, all inside measure A smaller kiln might be built, but the *proportions* should be the same Fig 2, is a fly or cone, to be placed in the centre of the spot where it is to stand, before the erection is commenced, the lower end, going into a hole, bored in a block of wood, fixed in the ground, the upper end, turning in a hole, bored in a cross beam, so that it is thus kept perpendicular, turning easily as the building of the kiln advances, thus the wall is formed internally of a regular sweep, without difficulty or trouble. The drawing-hole is two feet square, and the black dots denote the holes through which iron bars are to be thrust, at the time the kiln is charged, to prevent the fuel and lime-stones from dropping down, before the latter are properly calcined, these are removed as soon as the lime is sufficiently burnt at the bottom of the kiln, and it is afterwards permitted to fall, as portions are removed, the drawing thus being perpetual In charging the kiln, the drawing hole is to be filled with dry brush wood, then the bars are placed, and upon them are piled billets of dry wood, crosswise to the bars, and upon them, coal, if that be the fuel used, then, limestones about the size of the fist, and then, more coal, the fire is then lighted, and as soon as it has penetrated the mass, coal and lime-stones are thrown in alternately, until the kiln is full, taking care, however, to allow the fire to penetrate the last charge before another is added, or there will be danger of smothering the fire, and putting a stop to the regular combustion But before the kiln is

full, a portion of lime can be drawn periodically, as it becomes thoroughly calcined Should it happen, that the fire draws more on one side of the kiln than on the other, place stakes of wood in those parts where you wish the fire to rise, they will soon ignite, and the fire will follow them to the surface

These kilns are called *running*, or *perpetual* kilns, for as often as a portion of the calcined stone, or lime, is drawn from the bottom, alternate layers of coal and lime-stones are to be added at the top, so that the drawing and filling are perpetual If the kiln works well, one bushel of coal will burn about four bushels of lime-stones,* much, however, depends upon the nature of the stone to be calcined In stormy weather, it will be necessary to erect a temporary shelter to windward, on the top of the kiln, else the wind will press on the surface, and prevent the air from entering at the bottom, and thus the work will be much retarded, and at last, be ill done

The advantage of burning one's own lime is great, as you know I have burnt hundreds of bushels with the clearings of my wood lands, and peat and bushes and chips might be used for the purpose, provided care be taken not to impede the draught of air, the ashes, intermingling with the lime, and adding to its value If it be thought that the erection of a kiln is too expensive for one individual, a partnership might be formed amongst the neighbours, but it would be difficult to decide, who first shall have the privilege of burning, as all would often require the

* Refuse of colliery makes very good fuel for this purpose

8

lime 'at the same time , I, therefore, determined to incur the whole expense, and make the best of it

By kilns, like that above described, lime, to the amount of forty-five thousand barrels, of thirty gallons each, was burnt per annum, under my superintendence on the Forest of Brecon, South Wales, at an expense for labour, of five cents per barrel, it was carried by railroad about twelve miles, to the place of sale, where it brought twenty-seven cents per barrel, and was used almost exclusively for agricultural purposes, to the lasting benefit of a very large district of country , its effects, under all circumstances, being truly astonishing, but especially upon old worn-out meadows, causing white clover to abound where none ever grew before, this being its peculiar character

Frank But there is one advantage, or pleasure, in burning your own lime, which you have not mentioned

Father What is that?

Frank In being able to lend your kiln to your neighbours, when you do not want it yourself

Father That's good, it is fulfilling Scripture, you know, "It is more blessed to give than to receive"

Frank And that reminds me of the singular circumstance which took place, when Farmer Gannett came to offer to hire the kiln of you, after he had treated you in the dishonest way he did, and after trying to injure you, by breaking down your fences You, remember, he refused to have the use of your kiln, unless you would take money for it, and that you refused him the use of the kiln, unless he would

have it without pay , and what a struggle there was between you ! At last, he became melted by your kindness, and with tears, confessed that he had wronged you ! Now was not this, dear father, " heaping coals of fire upon his head," according to the true meaning of Scripture , melting him by kindness ?

Father You have delighted me, Frank ! And you know how often our neighbours have offered to rent it, after I have refused to take money, " splitting the difference," as they termed it, by proposing to keep it in repair for me, but I know the value of a good action too well, to part with it for so paltry a consideration as a few dollars a year ! to me, the opportunity of doing them service, is worth more than the sum the kiln cost in building, and I cannot part with it so cheaply, remember, "If ye do good to them that do good to you, what thank have ye" I knew an old close-fisted farmer, of whom his neighbour asked the favour of passing his upper field with his crop, which would shorten the distance to his barn, the old fellow hesitated so long, that at last, suspecting his neighbour would think him unwilling to grant his request, he replied, "certainly, I will give you permission to pass, but I have been considering whether there be not some way in which you can serve *me*, but as nothing strikes me at present, remember that you owe me a kindness" I have heard also of a lady, whose husband said to her, " My dear, I know you value yourself upon the close and saving manner in which you steer through life, but I know, likewise, that your neighbours and tradesmen do not respect you for it, now, for ten dollars a year, I will purchase for you one of the best characters in the town, *that*, I calculate, is about the sum which you save by extra management " I knew, too, a noble-minded old gentleman, whose son, his partner, wishing to overcharge an article in business, met from his father this memorable rebuke, " My son, don't sell your birthright to Heaven for a paltry dollar !

Frank. Now, I wonder if I shall ever be rich enough to be *very generous !*

Father. Oh, my boy ! don't stay until you are rich, before you are generous ! a generous disposition is worth all the riches in the world, for it will find the means of *gratifying its propensities*, as all other dispositions will We have known many men, who, all their lives, were accumulating riches, for the purpose of endowing some magnificent charity at their death such men have been justly charged, with holding on to their wealth as long as they could keep it, and then bestowing it, after it was no longer in their *power* to retain it, in a way to perpetuate their own memory !—selfish to the end ! While others there are, some of whom, blessed be God ! are still living amongst us, whose meat and drink it has been through life, to " go about doing good," who

" Do good by stealth, and blush to find it fame "

Never let the difference in their dispositions be forgotten, or the very different reception that awaits them, at that bar of account, which we are taught to

believe, awaits us all in another world Now, only just fancy one of these self-loving charitable characters approaching it after death, when the question might be asked, " what name?" answer " A B" " We have no entries on the credit side to that name " " Oh ! but I have bequeathed two hundred thousand dollars for charitable purposes " " Well then, you must wait, until we see how these charities are managed, and you will be held accountable for all the misuse that is made of your wealth, while fifty per cent will be deducted from all the *good* that is done by it, as belonging to those who have the labour of seeing your bestowment properly appropriated , so you must wait, and be held accountable You ought to have managed yourself, the talents committed to your trust, and been generous and benevolent during your life, laying up treasures in Heaven and not upon the earth , but you are not the only one, who has mistaken charitable endowments after death, for generosity and benevolence "

Now, compare this reception, with that which awaits *him*,[*] whose life has been one series of generous and beneficent actions, and to whose ancestor we are indebted, even for the pleasant shade of our streets ! who has *literally*, " gone about doing good," until the body is all but sublimed, but whose soul, like the setting sun, *seems larger as it declines !* And that blessed *saint*,[†] whose noble nature has placed her in the first rank of society, and to whom the

[*] John Vaughan, of Philadelphia whose father planted the trees around the State House
[†] Mrs ——, of Philadelphia, founder of the Ladies' Depository

8*

daughters, once of affluence, raise their streaming eyes, in acknowledgment of all the kind and generous support, extended to them in this, their altered estate! Oh! what strains of joy will resound through the courts above, when such spirits are welcomed with the heavenly salutation, *" Come, ye blessed of my Father !"*

Frank Well! here are heavenly portraits, but how indescribable the difference between them, and the endower of " a long row of alms houses !" I will be generous first, and then I will try to get rich, that I might be able to *indulge my propensities*

Father Our conversation has taken a singular turn, but it has been occasioned, I suppose, *by the mild and sweetening influence of the article which forms so large a portion of our compost heaps!* you see it has indeed, leavened the whole lump We will close by repeating those beautiful verses of Merrick's, which are ever present to my thoughts

> Blest, who with gen'rous pity glows,
> Who learns to feel another's woes,
> Bows to the poor man's wants his ear,
> And wipes the helpless orphan's tear !
>
> In ev'ry want, in ev'ry wo,
> Himself, thy pity, Lord! shall know,
> Thy love his life shall guard—thy hand
> Give to his lot, the chosen land
>
> When languid with disease and pain,
> Thou, Lord! his spirit will sustain,
> *Prop with thine arm his sinking head,*
> *And turn, with tend'rest care, his bed !*

DIALOGUE IX

GRABB

Frank Father, which is the most profitable breed of sheep for the farmer ? I should suppose the largest, for *as a sheep is a sheep,* you know, a large one must be of more value than a small one

Father A prudent man will advise with his land on that subject

Frank But, can his land advise with *him* ?

Father Yes, and the lessons which a farmer is taught by his land, are not soon forgotten, according to the old adage—" bought wit is best " I sometimes fancy that my crops converse with me, when I visit them of an evening, and if I could do justice to those dialogues which I seem to hear, and could commit them to paper, they would, I think, form a pleasant addition to your " book "

Frank O, do try, " nothing is impossible to a willing mind," you know

Father Most opportunely quoted, the *text,* now for the SERMON We will suppose, then, that a slovenly Procrastinator is visiting his fields on just such a glorious evening as the present, in just such a beautiful season, as we are now blest with He goes up to No 1, which is Wheat, and thus begins

Grabb. Good evening, fine weather this, but I don't think you look quite so well as you did the last time I visited you

Wheat. I wonder how I should, do you not see

how I am choked with weeds? how the thistles are goading me with their spikes, and the rag weeds are taking the food out of my mouth? while the bind weeds are dragging me to the earth, and how that I am smothered with evils innumerable

Grabb But I allowed you a fallow and plenty of manure, you ought, at least, to have been able to cope with the weeds

Wheat You forget that " the earth is own mother to the weeds, while she is only mother-in-law to the crops that are planted in her bosom," besides, you talk of a fallow—why this great thistle on my right and which has one of his spikes fixed in my side has just informed me, that he is one of the progeny, which was reared in this same fallow of yours, his parent being the identical thistle,* under which the farmer sat on horseback and escaped a drenching, while his neighbours were wet to the skin You seem to have forgotten, that " one year's seeding is seven years' weeding "

Grabb Ah well! I'll get these weeds pulled

Wheat. As you said a month ago, and will say again, and never do it

Frank Excellent! but you never fallow or dung for wheat?

Father Nor have I ever such fine thistles I always dung for green crops, and insure two things at the same time—more food for the cattle, and, of course, larger dunghills My object is, to retard the growth of the wheat, that it might grow strong in

* See page 26.

the stalk, and I do not, therefore, encourage its lavish growth, by manure and fallow Now for No 2

2 Corn.—Grabb Why you look very sickly, I thought you would do better, judging from the appearance you put on at first coming up, how's this?

Corn Ask yourself! You thought you were cheating me, when you sowed me without manure— a favour you always promised me—I relied upon that promise, and came up, with the expectation of finding it when I needed it, but after sending my roots below in search for it, I find your promises are false You complain of my sickly look! I can only say, if you had no more to feed upon than I have, you would not have shelled the three lower buttons on your waistcoat! Grabb tucked the shucks into the holes, and walked on

Frank I now find that crops can advise and admonish too, but could not the farmer still do something in the way of top-dressing, to remedy a part of the evil?

Father Yes, but he had no manure!

3 Barley—Grabb Ah! you'll come to nothing!

Barley I thank you, and return the compliment But what did you expect, when you sowed me after once ploughing on a stiff and wet soil? " Nothing venture nothing have," remember I only wish that *you* had to work so hard as I have for a living, you would then know how to feel for *me*

4 Oats —Grabb. Well, I think you might do a little better than you do, if you would try, why,

I sha'n't get the value of the seed back ! that's too bad

Oats Now, that's thrice bad of you ! You know that you have had six grain crops in succession, from the land upon which I am sown, with not a spadefull of manure of any kind for the last six years ! why, even the weeds have been starved out, and you have put in practice the lazy farmer's recipe for ridding the land of weeds—" make it so poor that they will not grow !" Now that's practical farming, without theory

Grabb. But what shall I do for want of the straw, which I depended upon as fodder for the cattle, during next winter !

Oats Is that the only dependence you have for next winter ? Why, your cattle will be ready to eat *you*, and you will have to practise the other part of the recipe, " to prevent cattle from dying of starvation—kill them !" But I give you warning, neither they nor you must expect any thing from me , if I can hold my own, 'twill be as much as I shall do

5 Clover —Grabb Why, you look healthy and well, but how is it that you have made such little progress in height ? there's Farmer Sykes' clover as high as my knees, and will soon be fit for the scythe, but I am unfortunate in every thing !

Clover That's a true word, although it is not spoken in jest Why, you seem to have forgotten that, as soon as I had made a little progress in growth, you turned in upon me all your starving cattle, horses, and sheep, which not only eat up the branch, but also the root !

Grabb Ah ! that I was compelled to do, to keep them from starving , but you had all the benefit of their manure, while they were feeding you

Clover. You call that manure ? why it was the greatest part, nothing but worms and bots , and the little good that remained, was soon carried off by the grasshoppers and bugs, which were about as much in want of it as I ! My fear is, that the hot weather, which seems now to be setting in, will scorch the land, so unprotected by foliage, and dry up the scanty crop which is left, before it is high enough for the scythe, and then, what do you think your horses will say to you ? If you had done as Farmer Sykes did, you would have deserved his success , you must remember, how, that instead of feeding off his young crop, he top-dressed it with a compost of lime and earth and dung, which had been carefully prepared during winter, and well pulverised , by which, not only his present crop is doubly benefited, but it is also preparatory to an autumn sowing of wheat on the lay Now put this and that together, and calculate the result First, two tons of hay per acre the first cutting , one ton per acre the second, with a capital aftermath for his dairy , and if wheat is sown by the 20th of September, a yield of forty bushels per acre might be expected at next year's harvest And this is not all, for after the wheat is carried, the land might be turned, and the clover stubble, perfectly rotted, will form an excellent seed-bed for turnips, with the expectation of an excellent crop. Now, I will leave you to calculate the value of *my* second crop, (remember you have already had my first cutting, and a severe *cutting* it was,) and of course you do not expect much at the third, while seventeen bushels of wheat per acre next harvest, will be quite as much as you have any right to expect, and common justice will not allow you to sow turnips after

Grabb Why, you are one of Job's comforters

Clover But I cannot see that you have any claim to the character of Job, for, " In all this, Job sinned not," remember

Potatoes —Grabb Well, I don't know how it is, but while others are digging new potatoes, it does not appear that I shall even have any to dig ! I may as well leave you to your fate, for you'll certainly never be worth the labour of cleaning

Potatoes Now you cannot be ignorant of the fact, that for two months after the crops of others were up, you were only *talking* of planting yours, and all the while, the weeds were growing on, what you termed a *fallow*, until some of them were as high as your head, we were then tumbled in together, and have ever since been striving for the mastery But you have now sealed our fate, and must take the consequences 'Twas fortunate for you, was it not? *that your father lived before you, for he would find it difficult to live after you !*

7 Cows in pasture —Grabb Well, *you* have more grass than you can eat, however, *you* can't grumble, that's certain

Cows Grass, do you call it !

Grabb Yes I do, and what do you call it ?

Cows Why we were just saying it would puzzle

a Philadelphia lawyer to say what it is, but judging by the smell as well as the taste, it might be called *garlic*, without offending against the statute of truth

Grabb Well, you are all alike ! didn't I let you feed off the crop of clover, almost before it was out of the ground ?

Cows That's fact ! indeed we were at last obliged to dig for it, and you will feel the effects next winter, or we are no conjurors

Grabb Ah ! I had need be a conjuror, to know how to satisfy you all, but what have you done with the sheep ?

Cows What, those large-bodied, long-wooled animals, for which you gave in exchange your small breed, which, *even they*, could only just keep body and soul together, by picking the short herbage of the pasture ? Oh ! *we* have done nothing with them, but they have been able at last to *do something for themselves*, for finding it impossible to subsist on such short commons, and that they were *growing less* every day, they sought for a hole in the fence, and by waiting until they were reduced so much in size as to be able to creep through, they at length passed into your wheat, with the intention of returning after they had filled themselves, but this they could not do then, and it is not probable that they have attempted it since, so you had better look for them, for ere this, they have cost you as much as they are worth, in the damage they have done to the wheat crop.

Grabb. Well, 'tis no use to try to do any thing more, and so I'll go straight home, no, not *straight*,

9

for if I do, I shall get amongst the porkers, and they are grumblers by profession.

9 Pigs—*Porkers* did you call us? 'twill be long before we have any *pork* about us, with our present mode of living, call us *grunters*, for so we are, and with reason, we wonder you are not afraid to meet us after dark, for we are but the ghosts of things that have been. There is one consolation, however, our lives will be spared, for we shall never be worth the expense of killing, indeed, that in a little time will be "no murder," it would be like one of your neighbours, who killed his pigs *to save their lives.*

Grabb Ah! well, here come the horses, they are the only generous animals upon a farm, but where are ye all going, in such a hurry?

10 Horses We have come at last to the resolution of no longer starving quietly, so we are going in a body, to break over the fence into Farmer Clement's clover, we know where the weak place is, for we have heard you promise, for the last three months, to get it mended, and *of course* it is not done yet. We do not intend to break into your own clover, as that would be punishing ourselves the next winter, for we calculate, there will not be more food than enough for us all, if we eat stock and block of the whole farm

By this time the farmer had reached his house, and going in, said to himself, "There is no comfort *out* of doors, let us see if we can get a little within Wife, bring the rum bottle and a pipe Talk of the independence of a farmer's life indeed, 'tis all a

hum—here am I, with the best intentions in the world—

Wife Not the value of a cent! all your *intentions* never grow into *actions!* Now, just sit down, and I'll sum up the *thousand and one* promises that you have made me, to do the necessary repairs about the house, and to begin with the roof of the dairy, which was stripped off by that storm last autumn, and there it remains in the same state to this blessed day—

Grabb *Take care! let me get to bed out of the way!*

Frank Oh! thank you! But now, to make a perfect picture, we should visit his fields with a good farmer and husbandman

Father That, indeed, would be much more agreeable, and some day we may do so, but it is now late, *let us get to bed*, as Grabb said, but not for the same cause, *blessed be God!*

DIALOGUE X

SYKES

Frank Well, father, you see the book is right— "nothing is impossible" When shall you be ready to give us the other side of that picture, which you yesterday drew for Grabb?

Father. The twin brother of the above proverb is, "nothing like time present"—by means of both, we may perform prodigies, so let us try at once. We will take our neighbour Sykes for the converse of the picture, and suppose him going into his fields to "meditate at eventide"

1 Wheat Ah! farmer, I am glad to see you, 'tis not often that you are absent for two evenings, I was afraid you were ill

Sykes Why you see I had promised my wife to attend to some little alterations about the house, and that has prevented me from seeing you as usual, we must take care of the women, you know, or they will care nothing for us, but *you* look well

Wheat Yes, thanks to your bounty I am now feeding on that magnificent coat of manure which you gave to the young clover last spring, and just at the time too, when it is needed, for if you will examine the plants on your left, you will find that the ear is already formed in the blade, and that they are all *five chesters* too

Sykes That's capital! now that comes of being *kind to the soil*

Wheat. And now, will you cast your eye over the ridges, and say, if you see any other piece of wheat in the country, so uniform and regular in its growth? The colour of the plants on the sides of the ridge, is, if any thing, of a deeper green than are those on the top, or crown of the ridge, a sure prognostic, at this season of the year, of a heavy crop The field below, is wheat, sown after a whole year's fallow and dung, but there the order is reversed, for the plants which are near the open furrows on the sides of the ridges, are weak and yellow, and will always remain so. And, only trace the rows of green spots, in straight

lines across the field! they were occasioned by the heaps of dung, which remained unspread for weeks, until they were overgrown with weeds, upon what was termed, a *fallow!* The weeds are now sturdy witnesses, that the dung and cultivation have done more for them than for the wheat, and yet, it is probable, that Farmer Grabb expects to reap a profit from his crop

Sykes I do not think that he will have either a *reap* or a *profit.* Your present appearance warrants an early harvest, by the blessing of a good season, and I am delighted with the prospect, can I do any thing more for you?

Wheat No, but there is something that you must do for yourself, you must increase the size of your stack yard I go for nothing less than forty bushels per acre

2 Corn—Sykes Well, I am glad to see you looking so much better, your first appearance was very weak and sickly, and my neighbours endeavoured to persuade me it was because I planted the seed with Buckminster's drill, but I knew *that* could not be the cause, for I never saw any machine operate better, I only wish the handles were longer, lower, and straighter, it would be more easily guided, and perform its operations with more ease

Corn My sickly appearance was owing to your own good management.

Sykes Why, how could that be?

Corn You know that you are in the habit of ploughing a *leetle* deeper every time, and thus a small portion of the sterile subsoil was brought to the surface, and in this the seeds were dropped, and the roller of the drill passing over—a capital invention—pressed them so closely into the clay, and rain falling immediately after, and following the track of the roller, the surface became so hard and dry, it was with difficulty I could penetrate it, and for a few days I looked miserably, I however soon reached to the manure below, which you had so bountifully supplied, and now, I feel as though I could mount to the height of ten feet! You may put me down for one hundred and ten bushels per acre I am in no fear of the weeds, which I see springing up around me, you'll take care of them, I know

3 Sugar Beets.—Sykes. Ah! Monsieur Sugar Beets, how you do? How you like our country and climate? how you like the *exchange!*

Sugar Beets Ah! Monsieur Farmer, I like your country! I like your fine, light and sunny days, they make saccharine I like the exchange too, 'tis all in favour of America But what for you not make sugar? make plenty sugar, more than in France, great remuneration! great and sweet recompense, no trouble, all pleasure, all profit

Sykes I do not consider that farmers in general ought to have any thing to do with the making of sugar, they can make beef and mutton and butter, and then they will afford to buy sugar, to their heart's content, leaving that branch of business to those, for whom it is so well adapted, to the capitalist and man of science, in whose hands there would be no fear for the result In the mean time, unlike most other speculations, the growth of the sugar beet in

this country, is about the most profitable business in which a farmer can be engaged, its enormous yield, forty tons per acre, insures food for all the living animals upon the farm Horses, cattle, sheep, hogs, and even poultry are fond of it, and better than all, it contributes, in a surprising degree, to the farmer's comfort, during the dreary time of winter, for it enables him to meet his animals without " fear and reproach," and gives him the means of fattening his stock at a time when others are starving, and he can rear house lambs too, which about Christmas would bring a fine price in the market In the introduction of this crop to notice, there has been no mistake, and for it, it must not be forgotten, we are indebted to " The Beet Sugar Society of Philadelphia "

In substituting this crop for barley, I have relieved the land of an exhausting crop, and have introduced one that is meliorating, requiring neither fallow nor dung *itself*—when the land is in good heart—but furnishing by its means, a mountain of manure for *others*, so farewell, Monsieur Sugar Beet

Sugar Beet Adieu, Monsieur Farmer, " Vive la republic America "

4 Potatoes —Sykes Well, the progress you have made in growth during the last two days surprises me! but never, for a moment, have I doubted the fulfilment of my most sanguine expectations, respecting this, my favourite crop

Potatoes But you have left us nothing to do but to grow, your labours began last autumn, when you ploughed the land deep, and laid it high and dry for the winter, and before others could get upon their land in the spring, you had planted your crop Then again, your judicious management in not moulding us up, we have only to go on to maturity, while the crops of those who keep moulding, never know where to be, or what to be at, for, just as they have discovered the height at which to form their bulbs, comes the hoe, and buries them so deep, as to ruin them, they are, therefore, compelled to form their bulbs higher, to be within the influence of the sun, leaving the first formed bulbs to their fate, but the plants, exhausted in a degree by the double exertion, are weakened, so as not to be able to bring the higher crop, any more than the lower, to perfection, and so, both are much reduced in quantity and injured in quality, producing many small and useless bulbs, happy, however, if they escape a third or even a fourth moulding Men are very silly, to suppose that potatoes don't know their own business best, the fear, that without moulding, they would form their bulbs on the surface of the ground, is very childish—why even *they* would not be so thoughtless and ignorant—their desire is, to find the spot where they shall be within reach of the sun's rays, and men need not fear they will get above it The crops that are not moulded up, are free from those half-formed bulbs or watery excrescences, which are so apt to deform those that are nursed into the rickets, and they form very few small bulbs, for the root is not anxious to produce more than it knows it can bring to perfection. By your excellent management, you will secure a harvest ten days earlier than your neighbours,

a crop larger in quantity and superior in quality, and which will command a readier sale and higher price in the market, put us down for seven hundred and eighty bushels per acre

5 Clover —Sykes Well, this is the finest crop of clover in the country, and will soon be fit for the scythe

Clover And no thanks to me, for you made me what I am, by that magnificent covering of compost, by which I was literally buried alive If the season proves favourable, I can promise you two tons of hay per acre the first cutting, one ton the second, and a capital aftermath for your dairy, and if that won't yield you a profit, why then quit, *and go a fishing !*

6 Cows in pasture —Sykes Well Fanny, Kitty, and Judy ! what have you done with Bill ?

Cows Oh ! he lies under yonder hedge, complaining *it is easier to lie down than to rise,* and thinks it hard to accompany us twice a day to the yard, when we go to be milked, indeed he will soon be too fat to be healthy

Sykes Well, I think you all live in clover, and the return which you make, of ten pounds of butter each per week, is a proof of your gratitude for good treatment

Cows We are very happy, and the proverb says, " Without comfort you can't make butter " But our happiness arises from your excellent care of us, especially, in dividing our pasture into three compartments, and changing it regularly, if men were but aware of the great advantage this is to the dairy, they would not compel their cows to lie in the same pasture until the very atmosphere is contaminated with their filth, the milk would keep fresh much longer, and the butter would not be so soft and so soon grow rancid in hot weather, to say nothing of the trifling circumstance, of about two pounds of butter a week from each cow, in favour of your plan

Sykes Well, I never heard cows talk so sensibly before! and I wish you would read Grabb a lesson on dairying, but unless he is the merest idiot alive, he must often have heard and read and felt the reproachful looks and low murmurings of his poor half-starved animals in the garlicky meadow below, but he is sunk so low, that it must be uphill work for him, I know

7 Sheep.—Sykes It is remarkable that, just as I had determined to dispose of my Leicester's, and purchase sheep of a smaller breed, more suitable for short pastures, that Farmer Grabb should decide upon parting with his Southdowns, on the principle that *as a sheep is a sheep, you know*"—(glancing his eye at Frank,) " a large one must be much more valuable than a small one," (Frank That's a hit at me ! I shall never forget the lesson which I have been taught,) so our exchange was no robbery

Sheep To us it was clear gain, but Grabb's sheep declare it was robbery—rank robbery, for they have been robbed, even of the means of existence

Sykes. To me, it has been very advantageous, and has proved the truth of the calculation " on

proportioning sheep-stock to land"—" The same land which carried indifferently, forty-five long wooled sheep, maintained in good plight, one hundred and fifty Rylands,"—small, short wooled sheep—I am, therefore, satisfied with the exchange

8 Horses.—Sykes But here come the horses. Well, my beauties ! why, where are ye going in that frolicsome mood ?

Horses Oh, we have eaten our supper, and are now going to rest in the upper pasture, we say to *rest*—Farmer Grabb's horses go to *labour*—for as they get no food after their day's work, they are compelled to gather their supper before they eat it, and hard work it is, with a bite so short, and after labouring at the plough all day, and all night at a short bite, 'tis no wonder that it costs him more in *whips* than in *corn* We shall therefore be ready by break of day, for whatever you will put us to for " with horses who are kept above their work, their labour is play "

Sykes Well, but take care now, and if you meet Grabb's horses down the road, don't go to play with them, for they have something more serious to think of Hallo ! where did that groan come from ? " And yet another, and another," as the man says in the play Oh ! 'tis only the hogs, who have overeaten themselves again, this is butter-making day, and they are always a little uneasy after that.

9 Hogs Ah ! and so would it be with you, if you had swilled so much as we have, but you men have no feeling for poor dumb brutes !

By this time, Sykes had reached the house, into

which he entered, singing the last verse of that fine old song, " No glory I covet," it runs thus

> " How vainly, through ignorant trouble and strife,
> The *many*, their labours employ !
> Since *all* that is truly delightful in life,
> Is what *all*, if they will, may enjoy "

Sykes Well, wife, your elegant supper table looks very inviting

Wife Frank, get your father's slippers

Sykes And my bettermost blouse * I mean now to " rest and be thankful " And, Frank, after supper, and while your mother and sister are plying their needles, you shall read to us " The Yellow Shoe-strings," which I read when I was a boy, and to the golden rule contained in that little book—" NOTHING IS IMPOSSIBLE TO A WILLING MIND," I owe the chief blessing of my life, don't I, wife ?

Wife Well, I confess that it had not been for your perseverance, the difficulties which opposed our union would never have been surmounted, and that, I guess, would have been unfortunate for all of us

Sykes Well ! after that, I think we may go to supper

Frank Thank you, father ! these stories will form a capital pair of portraits for my " book," and shall be preserved by me with gratitude, together with those remarkably beautiful lines which you gave me

---

* The French frock, a most convenient and suitable dress for a farmer

yesterday, and which have never since been absent from my thoughts

> For every evil under the sun,
> There is a remedy—or there is none—
> If there be one, try to find it—
> If there be none—never mind it

DIALOGUE XI

PRESSURE OF THE ATMOSPHERE.

Frank Father, I see no garden at all to be compared with ours for beauty and pleasure The shrubbery too, appears so large and the walks so long, although we know that the space which it occupies is but small, this must be occasioned by their winding course, so unlike all our neighbours' plans for laying out their gardens and pleasure grounds

Father You see that the walks in the shrubbery are, what are called *serpentine* , it has been decided, that " a curve is the line of beauty," and that, therefore, " Nature, which is all beauty, abhors a straight line " Now, in this, persons have been apt to overstep the bounds of moderation, and it is at length supposed, that walks for pleasure, cannot be made too crooked , they are mere snail creeps, and instead of " the swell of nature," we have the zig-zag of some clever man's brains Do you know, that the human figure can be drawn by taking segments of circles only—which mean curved lines—so that not a straight line shall be followed in tracing it?

Frank No, indeed!

Father. You see, then, the justness of the expression "the swell of nature," but this gentle swell, is very unlike the very crooked walks that are now so fashionable

Frank I have heard also, that "nature abhors a vacuum," but I do not know the meaning of this

Father A *vacuum*, means an empty space, and some persons, seeing that all nature is full and perfect, could account, in no other way, for the rising of water in a pump, when a portion had been drawn off, and an empty space or *vacuum* had thereby been occasioned in the pipe of the pump, into which, the water from the well would instantly rush, to supply it but it is the *pressure of the atmosphere* upon the surface of the water in the well, which forces it into the empty space, on the unerring principle, that every thing in nature *will find its level*

Frank How I wish to know more about the pressure of the atmosphere! I hear it often mentioned, but should like to understand it

Father It is by means of the air-pump, that persons have been enabled fully to understand the subject, this is a beautiful but expensive instrument, by which the air is pumped from under a bell-shaped glass, turned down on its mouth, just as though it were water You know that water is a fluid—so is air discovered to be

But we will endeavour to make a very simple

water-pump in about a minute, do you see this glass tube? I will show you by this, the way in which the pressure of the atmosphere operates Now, I will stop the upper end of the tube, and put the lower end into this pail of water, what do you observe?

Frank Why, the water has not risen into the tube —it remains empty!

Father The tube is already full of air, and it cannot escape, because I keep my thumb on the end of it, I will now unclose it, and see what will be the result

Frank The water rises into the tube, and is now just as high as the water in the pail

Father Yes, as soon as the air could escape, the water flowed in to supply its place, and has attained its level, this, as I said, is the law of nature, and is unerring Now, we will suppose this tube to be the pipe of a pump, and if we draw the air from the top of this pipe, there will be a vacuum formed, and the air, pressing upon the water in the pail, will force a portion of it into the pipe to supply its place in an instant See! I will draw off the air, by sucking it out.

Frank Ah! there it rises! but is not this sucking up the water?

Father To appearance it is, but it is merely drawing off the air, which permits the water to rise, and this could easily be proved to be the true state of the case, if this tube were thirty-two feet in height, for with all our *sucking*, or by any other power we could apply, it would not be possible to raise the water to a greater height than that. No common pump will draw or lift water higher than thirty-two feet, remember When you are older, I will take you to see what are called philosophical experiments, at present we must be content to examine and reflect in a plain way

Frank But I suppose that this might be called a philosophical experiment ?

Father Yes, and performed with a very simple apparatus too, it is enough, however, to show you the effect of atmospheric pressure on the water in a well, and the cause of the rising of the water in a pump

Frank Now, cannot you contrive to make an air-pump too ?

Father Let us try, our tin cup will make a decent substitute Fill it with *hot* water, and when it has stood awhile, empty it, and turn it down into the saucer, into which, pour a little water

Frank Oh ! how the bubbles are breaking out all around the edge of the cup, and forcing their way through the water in the saucer How is this ?

Father The air, which is confined under the cup, being rarefied or expanded by the heat, occasioned by the water with which it had been filled, forces its way round the edge of the cup, and through the water in the saucer, in bubbles, now, wait a moment, and take up the cup, and tell me what you observe.

Frank. Well, I declare! the saucer sticks so closely to the cup, that it is lifted up by it ! How did you contrive this ?

Father It was no contrivance of mine; it was caused by the *pressure of the atmosphere* Upon the

escape of the rarefied or expanded air from under the cup, none could enter to supply its place, because of the water in the saucer, which forms what is called a *water lute*. On the cooling of the cup, and consequent contraction of that portion of air which remained confined within it, a partial vacuum was formed, when, immediately the external air, being heavier than that smaller portion confined in the cup, pressed so forcibly on it, as to keep it fixed to the saucer

Frank. This is, indeed, a capital air-pump, and I now see how it is, that when a piece of leather, with a string fastened to it, is stamped on a smooth stone, it sticks so closely that the stone might be lifted by it! it is, because the air has been driven out from under the leather, and then the "pressure of the atmosphere" falls upon it, and fixes it to the stone

Father. It is so, and that you may perceive how we are surrounded with objects which call for observation, I will mention a very familiar example of the "pressure of the atmosphere," the effects of which cannot have escaped your notice You know that when we cross the line leading to Farmer Vince's house, we are in danger of losing our shoes by sticking in the clay?

Frank Yes, I have often done that, I know

Father The clay being soft, takes so exact an impression of the shoe, that at every step the air is driven out from under the foot by the "pressure of the atmosphere," and the foot is so forcibly pinned down, that it is often difficult to raise it And what is it, do you think, which presses so heavily the hot

10*

iron with which your mother smoothes the clothes after washing? the air is expanded by the heat, and is driven out from under it, when immediately, the external pressure on the iron, great in proportion to its heat, is sufficient to give one the idea of a copper-plate pressure

Frank. Our theory of haymaking, I declare *

Father. Exactly, and I am pleased with your application   I was going to say, take a cold iron, and press it with all your might, and you will scarcely make any impression , the same iron made hot, gives a pressure, equal to a mangle, heavily loaded , and this is increased by damping the clothes, as by that means, the expansion of the air is greater, and the vacuum thus created, more perfect   And see, how one observation leads to another   You have heard *London dirt* spoken of by those who have visited that city, and they declare there is no walking the streets, without splashing one's self from head to foot, the reason is this, the pavement is worn so smooth, and at every step the shoe fits it so closely, that the air is driven forcibly from under it, and then, the foot falls so heavily, in consequence of the pressure of the atmosphere upon it, that the mud is scattered about on all sides, as though it were *blown up* , while here, in the country, we can walk in the worst roads, without scattering the dirt, as the inequalities of the ground give space for the escape of the air, and support the pressure of the foot, by which all splashing is prevented

Frank   I wonder how many of the thousands who

* Page 52

crowd the streets of London, and complain of the mud, with which they are covered, ever think of attributing it to the right cause—*the pressure of the atmosphere*

Father   There is just one more instance which I will mention   You have often heard persons, who wear India-rubber shoes, complain of the pain which they experience, if they keep them long on their feet, especially in warm rooms   This is occasioned by the pressure of the atmosphere upon the feet, in consequence of the *vacuum* that has been formed around the feet by the tightness of the rubber shoes, which fit so closely, as to prevent any air from entering, to supply the place of that which has been forced out by expansion, caused by the heat of the feet, evaporation can therefore no longer go on, and the stockings and feet are often found wet with perspiration on removing the rubber shoes, while much pain in the feet, as also in the head, is oftentimes experienced during the time they are worn, the first, is occasioned by the pressure of the atmosphere upon the feet, the second, for want of proper circulation and evaporation, all insensible perspiration being checked, by the closeness of the rubber shoes, and I have no doubt much and serious illness has arisen from this cause.

Frank   Then, are not those water-proof clothes, now so much in fashion, injurious, from the same cause?

Father   Undoubtedly they are, and I speak from experience , for I once had a water-proof great coat, to defend me from the heavy rains to which I was at that time exposed, and was for some time at a loss to account for the extreme fatigue and lassitude which I always experienced on wearing it, until the thought struck me, that it arose from impeded circulation and checked perspiration, I never put it on again, nor ever again did I feel that sense of suffocation and difficulty of breathing, which always affected me when I wore it

Frank Thank you for this lecture on *the pressure of the atmosphere*, I shall now be able to account for many things which have puzzled me amazingly But there is still one, which I cannot understand, and although it does not seem to have occasioned much inquiry, it appears to me very wonderful, and I should like to know more about it I was reading in the Penny Magazine the other day, an account of the vast salt mines in Poland, which, although they have been worked for many ages, seem at this day, quite inexhaustible Other countries also, are found to contain mountains of this mineral in the bowels of the earth, while the never-failing salt springs, which are so often met with in this, and in almost every other country, might be supposed, I should think, to flow from beds of salt buried in the earth, and if so, they must be of infinite extent I used to think, this salt was different from *that* procured from sea water by evaporation, but it is proved to be identically the same, contaminated, sometimes, with other matters, but when purified, it is, in reality, *marine salt.* Now the question is, how came such enormous masses of

sea salt to be deposited at such great depths in the earth? Were they thus formed at the time of the creation of the world?

Father This is a most interesting question, and yet, strange to say, it would appear, that no attempt has been made to account for so wonderful a phenomenon Horne Tooke said, "What a man *troweth*, that is truth," and after much thought and reflection, I have adopted a theory—I suppose it might be called —which, although to my own mind it is satisfactory, yet I should almost despair of making it intelligible to others, much less, to render it plausible to any, but let us see what we can make of it

I believe, that the elements of this globe, earth, air, fire, and water, were all created at the same time, and are dependent upon each other, all being necessary for the formation of the *perfect whole* That the fires, which are raging at this time in the bowels of the earth, were kindled at the time of the creation, and that their grand office is *to furnish the earth with fresh water by distillation*—the water being originally *salt* That this salt water passes from the sea by secret channels, into the caverns of the earth, where, coming into contact with those subterranean fires, it is by them converted into steam, which, ascending through the crevices of the earth, is at length condensed into streams of fresh water, which form springs—the sources of rivers—upon the surface of the earth. The saline particles of the water, *which cannot be made to rise by distillation*, are left, after this process, in the bowels of the earth, the caverns formed by the burning away of the earth, becoming their receptacles, until they accumulate, so as to form those immense mountains of rock salt, which are there found at the present day, and from whence flow those salt springs, of which you have spoken   So then, thus it would seem, the waters of the ocean are continually escaping through caverns, (many of which we have read of, particularly that which forms the great whirlpool, *Maelstrom*, on the coast of Norway, a vast funnel, many miles in circumference, into which, if a ship enters, it is sucked or drawn down into the abyss, without the possibility of escape) when, coming into contact with subterranean fires, they are instantly converted into steam, which, on condensing, forms springs of fresh water. The residuum, *which cannot be evaporated*, goes to form those enormous mountains of rock salt in the earth, of which we have read.   Now, do you understand what I have been saying ?

Frank I believe I do, but the idea is so new to me, and so astonishing that I hardly know what to say   And yet, this theory seems to account, in a very natural way, for these mountains of salt, as also for those hot mineral springs in many parts of the world, of which we so often read, *boiling hot*, even upon the surface of the earth, and forced up to an astonishing height, by some invisible power; thus forming *boiling fountains*

Father Yes, and this theory accounts for the cause of earthquakes, and all those terrible revolutions, which are continually taking place in different parts of the

world, it would appear, that they are occasioned by the *power of steam !*

Frank Astonishing! we have here, at one view, the mighty power of that overwhelming agent ! and it is enough to overwhelm us with awe and wonder !

Father By this view too, we are enabled to understand how it is, that although " All the rivers run into the sea, yet the sea is not full," (Ecclesiastes, chap. 1. v 7,) as well as that, " Unto the place from whence the rivers come," (the sea) "thither they return again," for how can fresh water rivers come from the sea—the waters of which are confessedly salt—unless they have been first deprived of their salt, by some process, either in the atmosphere, or in the bowels of the earth ? and is it possible that this can have been effected by any means but by evaporation ? It appears, then, that the water which is evaporated by these internal fires, as well as that which is drawn up by the heat of the atmosphere, returns to the sea, to be again evaporated, to serve the same purpose, so that nothing is lost, and that this process has been going regularly on, since the day of the Creation !

O Lord ! how wonderful are thy works !
In wisdom hast Thou made them all

DIALOGUE XII.

SHEEP.

Frank Father, I was yesterday assisting John Lambert to drive his father's sheep to the upper pasture, and I could not help thinking of our late conversation, respecting the most profitable breed of sheep for a farmer In his small flock, you might find almost every variety, from the short wooled to the long wooled, with legs and bodies of almost any length, and necks longer than either! John told me, the long-necked animals were called aldermen's sheep, for it is a common idea in London, that on the day after an aldermen's dinner, necks of mutton rise in price, in consequence of the number that are then required for broth and thin soup, for those who had gormandized the day before! Some of these sheep certainly afford a rare opportunity for the anatomical lecturer, for their bones are about as easily defined, as those of a carcase fresh from the *hands of the ravens* I now see the truth and justice of the remark, that " a prudent man will advise with his land, on the most profitable breed of sheep for a farmer "

Father True, that might be called a practical lecture, not to be easily forgotten During a pretty long life, I have had opportunities of becoming acquainted with many of the different breeds of this most valuable animal, and as it might afford you instruction as well as amusement, I will endeavour to

recollect some of the most remarkable features of their character.

Frank " Features of character !" that reminds me of a paper in the September number of our monthly visitor, "The Farmers' Cabinet," under the head " A source of Comfort " I had no idea that we were so much indebted for our comforts, and even necessaries, to the simple and common article, *flannel!* but now, that the mornings and evenings grow cold, I am reminded daily of the gratitude which I owe, first, to " Him who doeth all things well," and next, to the interesting animals, who furnish us with the means of " defying the storm " I intend to copy the latter part of that paper into my " book"—it runs thus, " It is a most remarkable property of flannel, that although it prevents the *ingress* of cold, it seems, in a measure to facilitate the *egress* of heat, and is, on that account, admirably calculated to form the clothing of that animal, on whom alone, it might almost be said to be found , and which, without this wise ordination of ' Him who doeth all things well,' would be totally unable to move, or even to exist, under a covering from four to nine inches long, of a substance which, of the texture even of gauze, will enable a man to defy the elements! It is truly a wonderful ordination of nature, which ought to call forth, every day of our lives, the sacrifice of a grateful heart ! but the blessings of life, coming in the humble guise of a *flannel shirt*, are very apt to be overlooked , so true is it, that our greatest blessings are of everyday occurrence, and so common that,

11

MUTILATED PAGE

like the air we breathe, we might be said to *respire them*, too often with careless and unthankful hearts!"

Father Good, and now, as you remember I said, "a prudent farmer will advise with his land on the subject of the best breed of sheep," I will relate a circumstance which came under my immediate observation You have heard, that the Welsh mountains are famous for rearing a small race of sheep, whose carcasses always bring a very high price in the market at a certain season of the year, October, when they are slaughtered without other feeding, their flesh partaking of the flavour of the finest venison, from their having fed on the wild thyme and heath, growing on particular spots of these natural pastures, they are never slaughtered until four or five years old, when the mutton is very dark-coloured and full of gravy of the richest flavour—fit food for an alderman! Now, it so happened, that a very large tract of this wild mountain land came into the hands of a first-rate farmer, from one of the deep feeding counties in England, who could not bear the idea of rearing sheep, *even by the thousand*, to weigh no more than six or eight pounds per quarter, and he therefore resolved to introduce the improved South-down breed, of sixteen or eighteen pounds a quarter, determined, as he expressed it, "that they *shall do*" Now, the climate of this part of Wales, is wet, almost incessantly, and the Welsh breed of sheep, expressly calculated for such a climate, are covered with a loose, and rather long wool, which, separating along the back, falls over the sides, carrying off the rain,

and preventing it from penetrating to the skin, the South-downs, on the contrary, have extremely thick, close, and fine fleeces, not sufficiently long in the staple to divide and fall over the sides, so that, in such long and continued rains as are experienced in Wales, their wool becomes full of water, which penetrates to the skin, and soon causes the disorder called the pelt rot, in which, if you take the sheep by the back, the wool will separate from the skin, and come off by handsful, their fleeces are so close and thick, they cannot shake the water from them in rainy weather, whilst the native breed, will relieve themselves in this manner most readily

I remember this flock of South-downs, about two thousand in number, and some of the finest sheep of that breed I ever saw, coming to the mountains about Michaelmas, when the hills were covered with grass, of which there was no fear of want, even in the longest winter, and the owner had not, therefore, made any preparation for feed, except in mowing a portion of the long grass of the mountain, in the summer From the first day of their arrival, it was apparent to every one, that these sheep would starve, before they would eat an herbage, so entirely different from that short and sweet bite, which they had left upon the chalk hills of Sussex, where it is a proverb, "a sheep will grow fat on an eggshell full of grass a day," and on turning them into a pasture of five hundred acres, I do not think they ever stepped foot on fifty acres of the whole, unfortunately too, the weather set in wet, before they had recovered from a journey of one hundred and fifty miles, and sick and weary, they lay down amidst the long wet grass of the mountain, from which they could not be roused but by the dogs, while the rain, falling incessantly, would oftentimes form pools of water under them, in which they would lie and soak ! In a very short time, the wool began to separate from the skin, and many died, even before they had lost much of their good plight, which they had brought from their native hills

Frank But ought not the owner immediately to have removed them, when he foresaw the certain destruction of the flock ?

Father Undoubtedly he ought, but his pride would not allow him to do so. The Welsh farmers had foretold the event from the moment they arrived in the country, and were hovering around the dying flock—*like carrion crows*—enjoying the frightful catastrophe, and laughing contemptuously at the Englishman, who thought he knew so much more than they of the climate and country of which they and their forefathers had been the possessors for ages, and the owner of the flock had been heard to declare, he would lose every one of them before he would remove them, adding, " they *will* and they *shall* do " In a very short time they began to die by hundreds, and the shepherds had more than they could do to skin the dead animals, at last, their skins were no longer worth the labour of taking off, and then they were tumbled into holes, dug to receive them, as fast as they died ! I remember, after a dreadfully stormy night, I went to see the flock, early in the morning, and I shall never forget the horrid scene, thirty-five

had died during the night, and twice that number never again rose from their dying beds of long wet grass ! many of these last were lying under the dead sheep, still breathing, and the stench which arose from their putrid bodies, even before their death, was terrible ! I could not bear the sight or smell of mutton for a long time after

Frank Horrible ! but what was the end of all this misery ?

Father It only ceased with their lives, I do not believe that a single sheep escaped On the morning above mentioned, I was struck with the difference which then appeared between this flock, and one of native home-bred Welsh sheep, in the same pasture, these last had found shelter in the glens and behind the rocks of the mountain, and on my approaching them, would bound out of their hiding-places, shake the water from their fleeces, and set off on the gallop, to regain their companions, all life and vigour ! and one of them, having been left on this side a brook, which had become swoln to a torrent by the night rain, on running to it, hesitated a moment, and then plunged into it, and swam over to join his fellows, only stopping to shake the water from his dripping sides ! Do you now see, that " a prudent man will take counsel of his land before he determines on the breed of sheep he ought to keep ?"

Frank I do indeed ! " Experience keeps a dear school," truly

Father But the same person committed the same error, in the selection of his herd of cattle, for, from a deep and rich feeding county, he, at the

11*

same time, purchased about one hundred young, high-bred Durham cattle, which he turned upon the same mountains, to feed upon that coarse and poor herbage they did not die off so suddenly as did the sheep, as he took them into shelter during bad weather, but if my memory serves me, he lost about two-thirds of them before the spring, and sometimes as many as six of a night Now, the error proceeded from this cause the owner visited these mountains in the summer, and seeing loads of grass and never-failing springs of water, and the native breeds of both cattle and sheep in fine condition, it struck him that such fine pasturage ought to carry larger breeds of cattle and sheep, and judging from his success in the fine county he had left, he considered it was owing to a want of judgment on the part of the Welsh farmers, that they did no better, and having, very unreservedly, expressed this opinion, and boasted that he would soon teach them better, his pride, as I said, would not permit him to retrace his steps.

Frank Well, that is a frightful picture '

Father Then we will turn to another The occupier of a farm adjoining a residence which I once inhabited, was a man of the most perfect judgment in his profession, his horses, cattle, utensils of husbandry, &c, were of superior quality, but his sheep were his *hobby* ' he had spent a fortune in the improvement of the breed, and his annual shearing and sale of pure *Dishleys*, brought persons far and near to see his flock and *taste his mutton*, indeed they were beautiful animals, and as his farm was suited to deep keep, his flock was the pride of the country   It was

his custom, every Sunday morning to rise early, dress himself for church, a mile distant, and walk amongst his flock for an hour or two, examining every lineament even of their faces, feeding them from his hand, and conversing with them as with his children, while they, in their turn, would come to him to be fed and fondled !   I used often to accompany him on these occasions, and to him I am indebted for much information of real practical utility, and on these occasions I always thought of that beautiful verse—

> The husbandman goes forth a field,
> What hopes his heart expand '
> What calm delight his labours yield '—
> A harvest from his hand

I should say, his sheep were of the largest size, some of them having risen to thirty-five pounds per quarter, and I have known him to shear fleeces of nine pounds each in weight, but to bring them to this size and to keep their condition, it was necessary to provide them with, what is called *deep keep*, that is, cultivated crops, turnips, tares, clover, &c for all of this, however, they paid him handsomely, his lambs brought the price of his neighbours' full grown sheep, and no wonder then, his sheep were his greatest pleasure   An adjoining neighbour kept a flock of highly improved South-downs, and it was a question between them, which breed of sheep would pay best for fattening, an experiment was therefore made, by stall-feeding two of their largest wethers, weighing them at the time of putting them up, my friend beat his opponent by eight pounds per quarter

Frank Now that's a much more beautiful picture

Father Another excellent manager, who lived farther on the hill, and whose land was dry and pasture short, had the judgment to select his flock from the small South-down breed, but after holding his farm for several years, he found that by good tillage, his land had become able to carry a larger breed of sheep, he therefore crossed them with my friend's pure Dishleys, and with a single cross he obtained the kind of sheep which, I should say, was, upon the whole, "the most profitable for a farmer to keep" They were sufficiently large for every good purpose, sixteen or eighteen pounds per quarter, with the hardy nature of the dam, the fattening propensity and deep form of the sire, and the quiet disposition of both, with a fleece much heavier than that of the dam, and much finer than that of the sire, coming under the denomination of fine-combing, or coarse-clothing wool, suitable for both purposes They were capable of bearing cold and wet, and of producing a progeny full double the value of the dam, and of the most perfect form imaginable Indeed, I know of no sheep so generally suitable and profitable as a single cross between the Dishley and South-down, you know that the *Dishley, Bakewell,* and *Leicesters,* are the same sheep, under different names—they were originally bred by Mr *Bakewell* of *Dishley, Leicestershire* They are remarkably tractable in their dispositions, a necessary qualification in quick feeders

The success of Bakewell, in the improvement of the breed of sheep was very great, but it is now

admitted, that if he had commenced with *dam the best,* instead of *sire the best,* the end would have been accomplished in one half the time He once failed in business, in consequence of the great expenses which he incurred in pursuit of his favourite scheme —that of improving the breeds of horses, cattle, and sheep, for a handsome individual of either kind, he has been known to give the most extravagant prices, and used to boast that he never knew but one animal that money could not purchase, and that was a Flemish mare, for which he offered to give, just what her owner would ask, but nothing could induce him to part with her It was somewhat remarkable that, after making it a *sine qua non* that his sheep should have *no horns,* he bred his improved cattle with horns of frightful magnitude, hanging down by the side of the head, like, as has been said, *a great walking stick!* On the meeting of his creditors, at the time of his failure, he was permitted to select a ram from his flock, with which to begin the world anew His choice did not please his old and faithful shepherd, and a strife between them lasted four days, at the end of which, he gave up the contest, permitting the shepherd to make his choice, the event justified the choice, for from thence sprang the means of realizing a large fortune A butcher once purchased twenty fat sheep of Bakewell, and was to choose the best from a flock in a certain field, he did so, and took, with nineteen wethers, one of his most valuable rams, which had strayed amongst them, and slaughtered him immediately, boasting of what he had done! A prosecution was instituted against him, and damages, to the full amount of his property were awarded, after which, he was driven from that part of the country

Frank But I remember you told me, that your experiment to raise lambs twice in the year, was made by a cross between the Dishley and Dorsets, and the result must have been very satisfactory, I suppose, the lambs bringing such high prices, the first lambs selling for upwards of seven dollars each, the second bringing five dollars each, when sold to the butcher

Father It was just so, the second lambs were from the Dishley cross, very fine and large, the third lambs were from the same cross, and equally good. The first lambs brought such high prices, in consequence of coming so early—the Dorset breed being remarkable in this respect, still, however, I prefer the cross between the Dishley and South-down, for the purpose of stock

Frank I wonder if it was ever before known, that seven ewes brought twenty-eight lambs in the short space of sixteen months and a half?

Father Possibly not, but such was the fact, which can be verified by persons still living in the neighbourhood where the experiment took place

Frank I have heard and read a great deal of the Cheviot sheep, which are so highly valued as stock upon the Cheviot hills in Scotland, have you seen many of this breed of sheep?

Father I have, they were introduced upon the mountains in Wales, after the failure of the South-downs, and being longer and looser in the fleece,

more accustomed to high and exposed latitudes, and brought into the country during the summer, they were, in a measure, acclimated before the winter, and bore the change tolerably well, the Cheviot hills producing herbage, much of the nature of that on the Welsh mountains, still, however, they suffered dreadfully by the scab, which was, I am satisfied, occasioned, in a great measure, by the moisture of the climate and the injudicious mode of smearing with tar and grease—a management, introduced by the Scotch shepherds, who accompanied the flock from their native hills, and who, most erroneously, considered the practice of smearing, as applicable to the moist climate of Wales, as to the high and dry climate of the Cheviot hills The coat of tar and grease prevents the escape of insensible perspiration, and in a mild and wet climate, must have a most pernicious effect, and this was manifestly the case in Wales, for, soon after the smearing, the sheep lost condition, became loose and flaccid and large in the body, and the scab broke out so violently, as almost to ruin the flock, and totally the wool, for several years, and causing the death of many scores, indeed, for the whole of the time which I had them under my observation, the flock was never clean from the disorder of the scab, I have, however, heard, that they now do better, the smearing having been dispensed with Sheep can bear almost any degree of cold, if the climate be dry, the Scotch shepherds declared, they have experienced it so severe, as to kill the dogs while lying at their feet on the Cheviot hills, and yet, the sheep bore it well The Cheviots are a very pretty and useful breed of sheep, especially for high lands and coarse pasture, they are completely coated, even to the eyes and hoofs with wool, which enables them to stand the exposure of the mountain without flinching

Frank I have often heard of the sagacity of the Scotch shepherd's dogs, did you observe them to be particular in this respect?

Father I did, and have often been astonished to see them perform their *evolutions* At the time of which I am speaking, the number of Cheviot sheep on the estate, was seven thousand, these were divided into four flocks, and although they might be pastured on the same district, there was no danger of their intermingling, the dogs would guard against that The custom of the shepherds was, to remain with their flocks until they had lain down for the night, and then, to leave them until a little before daybreak in the morning, when, on going quietly amongst them, they knew, to a certainty, if any one was sick, for it a sheep does not stretch itself on rising, it is a sure sign of disease But, before disturbing them, the dog would take a circle round them, to ascertain by the scent, if any strange sheep had visited the flock during the night, and if there had, he would go into them and seize the straggler by the cheek Towards evening, the shepherds were accustomed to collect their sheep into a circle in some sheltered spot, if a storm was apprehended, and to do this, it was only necessary for him to say to the dog, *go round them*, when away he would start, circling them so quietly, and at such a distance, that

they would continue to feed all the way as they approached the shepherd, who had thus again the opportunity to examine and count them, to ascertain that all was right for the night, and if he observed any symptoms of sickness, he had only to point out the individual, when the dog would go so quietly, and take him by the wool of the cheek so gently, as scarcely to disturb the rest of the flock, after this, the shepherd had only to remain until they were lain down, when he could leave them, with the certainty of finding them in the same position in the morning at daybreak. Some of the pastures were bounded on one side by a wall, and on the other by a bank, and if, on removing the flock, the shepherd wished to head the sheep to the right or to the left, he would say to the dog, *over the dyke*, or *over the wall*, and he would never mistake the one for the other At the season of lambing, each shepherd was furnished with a stone bottle, strapped across his shoulder, and filled with cow's milk, for the support of the lambs lately dropped, and which were, perhaps, too weak to suck their dams, and the way which they administered this cordial was curious, they would take a large mouthful of milk, and keep it there, until it grew warm, then, clasping the lamb between their knees, and opening its mouth with the fore-finger, they would permit the milk to run from their mouths in a small stream, directly down the throat of the lamb, in the most convenient manner possible

Frank I have heard also, of the disease called the *merino-mania*, do you remember the time when the

12

whole people seemed, all at once, to be affected by this cruel disorder?

Father Perfectly, and it was indeed a "caution" to observe its effects, even on sober-minded people! and no need of the excitement either, for if the merino cause had been taken up by those only, to whom, as a business it properly belonged, nothing would have succeeded better, or have been attended with better results, but all must dash into the speculation, and I have heard that even merchants' clerks would have their *merino*, tied up in, perhaps the *coal-cellar*, by which they calculated to make a profit of one or two hundred per cent! It is a most valuable breed of sheep for some purposes and situations, and with care and attention, have been found to retain all their distinguishing properties, and greatly to improve in the article of mutton, in which they were originally deficient They were introduced into England by George the Third, who, at great expense and trouble, imported them direct from Spain, for the improvement of the wool for clothing purposes It was his wish, to place them in the hands of those most likely to take the greatest care of them, and he therefore made presents amongst the nobility and great flock masters of England—but all fell through—none could be found to take the necessary care of animals which came into their hands so cheaply, and it was the happy thought of Sir Joseph Banks, to sell a portion by auction, considering that when men paid dearly for *their whistle*, they would take care of it Accordingly, in 1808, the average price of ewes at the

king's sale was £23 12s 6d, of rams, £33 10s 1d the highest price for a ewe being £38 17s, of a ram £74 11s and then came *the tug of speculation!* Every one thought that merino wool would eventually be the only article grown, and upon this, therefore, the people would soon have to depend, for life and breath and all things! In the mean time, a few persons of judgment and skill, set themselves quietly to examine the matter, and amongst the first of these must be placed, Lord Somerville, and Dr Parry, in their hands, these sheep proved to be all that they had ever been led to expect, and although at first, the wool dealers and clothiers were determined to consider the wool of the anglo-merino sheep, inferior to the imported Spanish, yet Dr Parry, by a singular method, convinced them against their will, and condemned them out of their own mouths! It is said, that for several years, he packed the wool of his anglo-merino flock, in the bags which had been emptied of the purest imported Spanish wool, bearing the mark of the paular flock—Refina—and introduced it into the market *as such*, readily obtaining the highest prices of the day, without a suspicion of its being the growth of England! and these prices had risen, in the year 1809, to the enormous sum of twenty shillings English per pound This plan, it is said, he adopted, because he could not obtain of the wool buyers, a price at all equal to the value of the article, but by it, the sales were easily effected at a price equal to that demanded for the prima piles of imported Spanish And he obtained a premium from the Bath Agricultural Society, at their annual meeting, at which the committee reported as follows. "They had, in conjunction with several woollen-drapers of the city of Bath, minutely inspected the comparative quality of cloths, Nos 1 and 2, and had adjudged, that No 1 was entitled to a preference, in respect of fineness of wool," (it appeared on examination that No 1 was manufactured from the wool of Dr Parry's anglo-merino flock, and that No 2 was made from one of the best piles of wool imported from Spain, and known by the name of the *coronet pile*) "And they were decidedly of opinion, that Dr Parry had accomplished the grand object of producing, in the climate and soil of Britain, wool equal to that imported from Spain " Now, this object would not have been accomplished, had not the sheep been sold for enormous prices, when they were *given away*,* no one cared much about them, and they were consigned to the care of servants, who, generally speaking, entertained strong prejudices against them, and at best, were not sufficiently careful to prevent them from becoming contaminated with other breeds

And here I cannot resist the mention of a circumstance, which was related to me by my friend, the Dishley breeder He said, "I once attended an agricultural meeting, of which the great Arthur Young was president his speeches filled all with enthusiasm, and led us to consider a visit to his farm, which was

* It is a fact, that at the first introduction of the seed of the French sugar beet into this country, by " The Beet Sugar Society of Philadelphia ' some of the first agriculturists of the State, declined accepting it as a gift '

in the neighbourhood, as the greatest treat we could enjoy, as there, we were sure to witness all his theories carried out to practice I therefore obtained his permission to visit his farm the next day, with a letter to his shepherd, instructing him to show me every civility, and permit me, especially, to examine his flock The next morning early found me on the road, enjoying, in anticipation, the pleasure of seeing an establishment built and supported by long experience, consummate skill, and the most ample means of improvement—but how shall I express the mortification which I experienced! A fine farm cross-cropped, and badly managed, was nothing to the *horror* which I felt when the shepherd introduced me to the flock of sheep, which had been brought into an enclosure for my inspection They were of all sorts and sizes—ringed, spotted, and speckled—dirty, draggled, and dingy—with ewes and rams promiscuously mixed The shepherd, seeing my surprise, mistook it for excess of admiration, and began to launch out in praise of the objects of his care at last, I requested him to point out the best and most valuable ram in the flock, upon which, he seized upon a huge thing, and dashed him down on his rump, in a way which he should not have used one of my sheep for his head, and asked if I had ever seen his like I answered, No, indeed! but pray be so good as to show me what you consider his most beautiful points,' upon which he looked up and said, exultingly, 'Did you ever see such a *nostril* in your life?' Now, in this sheep I thought I could point out every defect that I had ever witnessed, his

12*

fore-legs reminded me of a pair of scissors, and I could have buried a loaf in the hollow behind his shoulders! his head was tremendous, but oh! his *nostrils!* they did indeed throw all his other defects into the shade! I never attended any more agricultural meetings where that honourable gentleman was president"

Frank Well, here are varieties of sheep, from whence a judicious farmer might make his choice, and upon which, I perceive, his future success must, in a great measure, depend, and I now see that *size* ought not to be the only criterion by which to judge of the most suitable breed for the farmer The nature of the fleece—a circumstance often overlooked—must be of great consequence in many situations, while the profit of the flock cannot be confined to any one particular breed I have heard it said, a certain farmer, who lived near a large town, bred his sheep heaviest in the hind-quarters, as that part of the carcass brought a higher price in the market than the fore-quarters, and on the butchers complaining that the sheep had not much " inside fat," he replied, " Only let me know how much you want, and I'll soon make it for you," and this he did, by crossing the breed

Father Yes, and my friend, the Dishley breeder, used to say this could easily be accomplished for " If you wish to have inside fat for the candle makers, breed your sheep narrow across the back, and you'll be sure to have it, all the juices flow to the back, and remain there, if the animal is wide across the back and loins, if narrow, however, they pass away

and settle in the belly and offal of the animal—but I profess to grow mutton, not *soap and candles!"*

As an application of this our long conversation, remember that there is a *fitness in all things,* and to be able to choose the most suitable rank in life, as well as the most valuable breed of sheep for the farmer, we must take counsel of our *means* as well as our *land,* not expecting too much in any one variety, or in any one situation the merits and advantages of all combined In our situations in life, all the advantages are not confined to one particular sphere, be it ever so prosperous in appearance, and if the truth could be known, I believe it would be found that we are much nearer upon a par, with regard to the blessings of Providence, than most persons imagine I cannot afford to *keep a carriage*—true, but, blessed be God! I can walk—which is more than Sir John D—— can say, for if he had no carriage, he could never more enjoy the pleasure of fresh air and exercise I do not possess riches—true, but I enjoy all that is requisite to constitute happiness, and I am reminded of a very rich man to whom a person applied for charitable assistance " Why," said he, " you say you have food and raiment and lodging—and I assure you that is as much as I get, amidst all my seeming superfluities" And I once knew a farmer who was as happy as a long summer's day while he occupied the farm at A——, but when he became a gentleman, and retired from business, in consequence of the great wealth of which he became so very unexpectedly possessed on the death of a distant relative, who had amassed it in India, he grew so wretched, that "it would be a sin to wish a dog such a state of existence," as a friend expressed it who had visited him at his mansion, and found him in a little dark room, with his hat pulled over his eyes, and rocking himself, almost in a state of frenzy! My friend said he uttered these memorable words—"You knew me at the farm of A——, a hard-working man, but contented and happy—you now see me a wretched being, without a comfort in the world! The grasshopper is a burden to me—and all this misery arises from this cursed wealth!" Poor wretch! he died soon after, and the neighbours declared that his days and nights were so haunted with frightful shapes, that his death was the only happiness remaining to him! nor could they believe but that his misery arose from the *kind of wealth* that he possessed—remarking, "Lord C—— and his steward returned from India loaded with gold—*he* shot himself in his mansion, and the next morning his steward was found hanging by the neck in the chalk-pit above the house!'"

Now, compare these men, in all their glory, with such a man as our neighbour Sykes, with his cheerful temper, kind feelings, and generous disposition, and the contrast will be striking indeed! With a cool head and a warm heart, expanding as it does "at sight of others' wo," I know of no one more noble, or that stands higher in the estimation of every one, be his situation in life what it might he is a fit companion for the first man in society, and a warm friend

to the most destitute, while the order and regularity observable in all that he does, is the admiration of every one You know how peculiarly neat is every thing about him, and the elegance which is displayed in the fitting up of his little parlour as a library, especially the plan which he has adopted—that of making every year a map of his farm, and designating the crop of every field by colours, and figures of reference, and suspending it above his mantel-piece as a picture, framed and glazed, and above all, his journals for every year, which contain every circumstance of importance that has transpired in that time, and to which he can turn in a moment—indeed, I know no one like our neighbour Sykes

Frank Oh, father, how I wonder that every farmer does not keep a journal in which to enter every evening whatever of importance has happened during the day, as well as to record the result of experiments, which might be made in the way of improvement of stock or crops, the times of sowing as well as the times of harvest, with many other circumstances that would gather additional interest from comparison with passing events It is very pleasing to witness, when we pass an evening with farmer Sykes, or he with us, with what eagerness you turn to your journals, to prove the correctness of a *surmise* that might have employed you, perhaps, for half an hour, when in a moment there appears *chapter and verse*—for or against—that sets the question to rest at once On looking over one of your journals the other day, I found a very particular account of the experiment which was conducted by you, to ascertain the truth of the assertion, that ewes of the pure Dorsetshire breed would produce lambs twice in the year * I should like to copy that account into my " book," as the record of a most remarkable circumstance

Father Do so, by all means It is a fact in the remembrance of many yet living in the neighbourhood where the experiment was made, and is still considered, as you say, a remarkable circumstance But you must not suppose that it is merely the number of the lambs so raised that is unprecedented There is a breed of sheep in some of the western counties of England, which almost always bring twins, and often three lambs at a birth, and I remember, at the time while I was conducting the above experiment, meeting a young farmer in Devonshire, who assured me he had at that time a small number of these sheep, which he kept by way of curiosity, and which had then almost all twins, and five of them three lambs at a birth ! He, however, did not value them for any other purpose, as they were small, coarse, ugly, and valueless—remarking, "One might almost as well keep a flock of cats, which would bring twice as many at a birth" He said there had been instances of these sheep bringing four at a birth

Here, then, is a particular account of my experiment, which was conducted for the purpose of ascertaining the truth of the assertion, that the pure bred Dorsetshire ewes would infallibly produce lambs twice in the same year My friend, the Dishley

* See page 130

breeder, taking an equal interest in the question, furnished me with one of his most valuable Leicester sheep, as a cross, and I commenced by purchasing seven ewes on the second day of December, 1825 They were all in lamb, and by the twenty-eighth of that month had yeaned nine lambs The first of these ewes lambed the second time on the second day of July following, in the year 1826, and the remaining six by the twenty-sixth of the same month, bringing seven lambs They were all in perfect health, the lambs remarkably strong and fine, a cross with the pure Dishley breed My neighbours were surprised, but could not believe that the ewes would lamb again in the following spring, and considered the thing quite settled that if they did, I should not then have any twins but by the fourteenth of March, 1827, five of them had lambed the third time, and the remaining two by the twenty-ninth day of April, producing, at this lambing, *twelve healthy lambs !* Thus, seven ewes, in the space of seventeen months from the time of their purchase, produced twenty-eight lambs, which were all reared in safety, and were sold, the first crop to the butcher, for seven dollars each, the second crop to the butcher likewise, for five dollars each, and the third lambs were sold with the ewes as couples for stock

This has been a long story, but it is on a subject of great importance to those who are engaged as we are in life The employment of the shepherd is one of the most ancient on record, and the continual reference to this very pleasing occupation, which we find in both the Old and New Testament, has en-

deared it to many who have never enjoyed, as we do,
the pleasure in reality   Let us close by reading that
beautiful versification of the twenty-third Psalm

> As the good shepherd gently leads
> His wandering flocks to verdant meads,
> Where winding rivers, soft and slow,
> Amidst the flowery landscape flow—
>
> So God, the guardian of my soul,
> Does all my erring steps control,
> When lost in sin's perplexing maze,
> He brings me back to virtue's ways
>
> Though I should journey through the plains
> Where death in all its horror reigns,
> My steadfast heart no ill shall fear,
> For Thou, O Lord ' art with me there '
>
> By Thee with peace and plenty blest,
> My life is one continued feast,
> Thy ever-watchful providence
> Is my support and my defence '
>
> O, bounteous God ' my future days
> Shall be devoted to thy praise,
> And in thy house, thy sacred name
> And wondrous love shall be my theme '

DIALOGUE XIII

CULTIVATION

Frank Father, our conversation on pruning has
never been absent from my thoughts , it has indeed
proved, as you said it would, a source of great delight and instruction to me   I often visit the tree
which you pruned at the time, and am astonished to
find how very correct were all your ideas, respecting
the manner in which that work ought to be done,
and how true to nature is the similarity between the
cultivation of trees, and the management of children
—some of which might be *pretty big ones too.*

Father The more you reflect upon and examine
the subject, the more interest you will feel, and the
clearer will be the truth of the observation

Frank I have no doubt of it, for I find myself
making new discoveries every time I visit that tree ,
it might be said to be a *living lesson*

Father Good , and do you ever remark the three
branches, which we particularly noticed at the time
of pruning, and which we named William D John
Timms, and Sister Susan ?

Frank Indeed I do, very particularly, and cannot
help thinking they were excellent likenesses   The
fine large branch, so tall and so straight, which, when
you headed down, I thought you had spoilt the tree
for the whole year, has, from the part which remained attached to the tree, thrown up two beautiful
branches, one on each side, like twins, exactly of the

same height and size, of a deep red colour, which, I
have heard you say, is a sign of fruitfulness, and
they are clothed, to the very foot of the stalk, with
buds and leaves at short distances, and that is, I
believe, another good sign, and more than that, they
are shooting up into a part of the tree, which before,
was thin of branches, filling the vacancy, and rendering the tree very much more beautiful than it
ever could have become, had that branch remained
in its original state These new branches are indeed,
as you said they would prove to be, "useful as well
as ornamental, affording shelter to their parent, instead of shooting above, and out-topping the tree,
exposed to every blast that blows" What a pity,
that William D's mother had not received the benefit
of such a lecture "on pruning" in her youth!

Father But what did you remark of poor John
Timms? Do you think he is the better for the training which he received?

Frank I was just coming to him, he still shows
that he is too willing for his strength, for he is loaded
with fruit from the bottom to the top, and which it is
not possible can ever be brought to perfection. I
suppose you will have to pluck off more than one
half The appearance of health and strength is,
however, much increased and although the branch
will always remain, like poor John, deformed, yet
by careful and kind treatment, it might long continue one of the most useful, although not the most
ornamental branches of the tree, a living proof of
the value of judicious training

Father. Well, now for Sister Susan

Frank Oh, sweet Sister Susan! indeed, indeed
the likeness is complete! there is the pretty red
branch, and the beautiful shining leaves, with fine
fruit peeping from beneath them, all of the same
size, and growing exactly where they ought to grow,
with the red and white so sweetly mixed, although
still so small in size, with a leading shoot from the
top of the branch, covered with leaves, without
blight or canker or mildew! Oh it is pleasant to
look upon, this comes of good training

Father But is there any hope of a Frank on the
other side of the tree?

Frank There is, and the first time I saw the bud
bursting from the body of the tree, I confess that I
was quite overcome by my feelings Oh, shall I not
watch its progress, and witness its growth and tendency with anxiety!

Father Let but my prayers be granted, and I shall
have abundant cause for rejoicing

Frank But, father, is not the growth of the tree
dependent, in a great measure, upon the kind of soil
in which it is planted?

Father There, my boy, you have laid open a large
field for observation and reflection, and suppose
now, we follow it out, and see if it be not true, that
"the growth of the tree is influenced, in a remarkable degree, by the nature of the soil in which it is
planted" Shall we divide the different qualities of
soil in the following manner

1st The happy soil neither too heavy nor too
light, too wet nor too dry

2d The heavy soil

3d   The too light, or sandy soil.
4th   The wet soil
5th   The dry and impenetrable soil
6th   The rich surface and sterile subsoil
7th   The poor surface, and rich subsoil
8th   The sour and stubborn soil
9th   The rich soil, with poisonous subsoil and,
10th   The sickly, or too highly manured soil

Frank Well, here are varieties of soils! Shall we be able to fit them all with *likenesses*, do you think?

Father Many of them will be easily matched I believe. And to begin with

1st   The happy soil, which requires neither liming, manuring, draining, nor watering, whose excellent properties are so nicely blended, and whose productions are so beautiful, rich, and in such profusion, can any thing be more like the founder of the Widows' Asylum?

Frank Oh, excellent, a real portrait!

Father 2d The heavy soil, which produces a thick and burly bark, short, coarse, rough leaves; with short, crooked branches, and fruit, although of a healthy growth and colour, with no delicacy of flavour, bitter to the taste, with large stones, to which the flesh of the fruit adheres very closely, the tree comes late into bloom, and the fruit ripens late, but it is generally a good bearer of fruit, *such as it is* Now who is this? or shall I name him what do you think of Tom Dobbs, on the other side of the hill?

Frank As like as life! even to the shortness and roughness of his limbs, a hard-working man, but

rough and brutal in his manners, and although he provides for his family as a duty, to the pleasure of the task he must be a perfect stranger, his children are coarse in their manners and sour in their dispositions, and are never sent to school hard workers, however, and they produce much fruit, *such as it is*

Father Very well, now shall we cultivate the soil as we go? This tree requires but little pruning you will observe, as it produces but little wood, all that it does produce, however, it ripens well

Frank Yes, let us cultivate as we go now how would you set about it in this case?

Father It would be merely to trench about the tree, dig in a good quantity of sandy loam, with lime *as a sweetener*, and depend upon it, in a year after, the results would be manifest, a more open disposition, warmer feelings, sweeter fruit, a more luxuriant foliage, and a *smoother bark* Now for

No 3 The too light, or sandy soil This is indicated by a tree of a weak and sickly aspect, long and thin branches, very thin and light-coloured leaves, comes early into bloom, and is very apt to blight in the spring, if the season is cold, it sometimes however, escapes, and then it brings an early crop of sweet fruit of little flavour During the summer it throws out much thin and long wood, which is sure to die back in the winter, rendering it necessary, the next spring, to head down almost every individual branch It sheds its leaves early in the autumn, and its weak limbs are very liable to be broken and wounded by the storms of winter Now who is this?

Frank Oh! I know that, it is Samuel Shmm, the tailor in the village, and is it not like him? You know how tall and slender he is, and how sickly he looks, and how thin and sandy-coloured his hair, active and industrious, but complains of the steepness of the hill behind his house, and is not able to leave his home until the season is warm, and the cold weather has passed; civil and kind-hearted, but with little energy, either of body or mind while, on the approach of winter, he keeps to the house and suffers from every change of climate Now, you must be gentle in the cultivation of so tender a subject

Father Yes, I would trench up the sand, and mix with it a large dose of strong loam and lime compost, prune very close, leaving but about three buds on each branch, and *look well to the worms*, which such a weak and sickly subject is pretty sure to be infected with

No 4 Is the wet soil, a most unhappy soil truly! It is shown by strangely formed branches, sometimes smooth and straight, at others, crooked, burly, and rickety, with leaves of different sizes and shapes, smooth or wrinkled, green or yellow, thick or thin, just as the season happened to be during their growth, the tree generally glutted with too much moisture, and in a happy state, only when others are parched with drought, nothing more uncertain than its fruiting, sometimes producing largely at a time of general failure, and barren in the most fruitful season The wood which it makes during the summer, dying back almost the whole of its length, but shooting again vigorously from the first living buds in the spring,

sometimes healthy to appearance, with large promises of productiveness seldom realized Now see if you can find any one so unfortunately situated in life

Frank Well, to be sure it is a wretched picture, and yet I think, poor James Snooks the shoemaker, is the pitiable object. You have often remarked as he passed, that he is the strangest being you ever saw, lively in a time of sadness, and gloomy and sad at merry-makings always preparing to do great things, but failing, just at the time when great exertion is necessary, sick, but not sorry, sorry, but not sick, doing more work in a week than any one, and less in a fortnight than all, joyous, grievous, bright, and gloomy all by fits and starts Now, how could any thing be done to recover so pitiable a case?

Father It would, indeed, require a *regular course of medicine* and strong measures, but even here I should not despair of perfect success I would fairly remove the tree, clean the roots, dig out the earth to a great depth, and if on a declivity, I would drain the soil, if on a level, fill the hole with about eighteen inches of brick and mortar rubbish, and well ram it down, and upon this I would spread a thick bed of good mould and lime, replace the tree, and support it by tying it to stakes with hay ropes, and my life for its recovery, looking well to the worms, however

Frank Well, these would be decisive measures, at any rate.

Father Yes, and would be decidedly efficacious

No 5 The dry and impenetrable soil, shows a tree, poverty-smitten in all its parts, unable to do much, nor that little to any good purpose, brisk and lively, however, in early spring, and making exertions to push into bloom and leaf, but cramped and spell-bound midway, the under leaves fall prematurely, but the wood which it makes during the summer, is retained through the winter, although but little of it, stunted and bark bound, but healthy in a degree, and not liable to be affected by the worms, for that reason Now this is so common a character, that we have known many such, who are truly to be pitied To recover such a tree, it is only to "dig about it and dung it, and let it stand another year," adding however, a good portion of lime with the earth, on filling in

No 6 The rich surface and sterile subsoil, frequently to be met with, and often the cause of disorder, disease, and death, to the tree that is planted in it, the richness of the surface-soil, calling forth early spring foliage, and the most promising expectations, the sterility of the subsoil, causing a lamentable falling away of the brightest hopes, and the most grievous disappointment In early youth, it is lavish of foliage, and the sweetest blossoming, all appears well and as it should be, and no one would suspect the mortification which is sure to follow, when the roots have penetrated to the poverty-stricken soil below Now this is a character which is, unhappily, very common, and is aptly figured out in the case of William D in our former conversation Hundreds of such young men, reared in the rich surface-soil of parental affection, their cultivation neglected through a mistaken fondness, after giving promises of the

most enviable greatness, are doomed to poverty, disgrace, and contempt, through the want of the *proper stirring of the subsoil*—the only security for parental hopes Such cases require a strong hand nothing less than a regular trenching will be of any avail, the rich surface should be turned down, and the sterile subsoil be brought up, to be enriched by future dressings, lime forming a large proportion in every stage of the business, for it is much to be feared that the worms will be found to have made sad havoc near the root of the tree, as disease, arising from the poverty of the subsoil, will, in all probability, have engendered life Lime and deep trenching will, however, heal the malady, if applied in time To this disease is owing the change of the colour of the leaf before autumn, and the falling of unripe fruit, with many other symptoms of premature decay

No 7 The poor surface and rich subsoil are also very common, and before the tree can reach the good soil beneath, poverty has stricken it, and many there are which perish for want of sustenance, not having strength sufficient to reach the buried treasure, they languish, for want of support, and without timely assistance are doomed to starvation, we may find many semblances to this case I fear, amongst the children of the poor and friendless, for, according to the poet,

"Full many a flower is doomed to blush unseen,
    And waste its fragrance in the desert air"

Frank Yes, and I know one who is so unfortunately circumstanced, it is poor George Hastings, the apprentice to the blacksmith, how I pity him, when I see him drawing figures with chalk upon a board, and hear him sigh because he cannot read! while his brutal master checks every attempt at improvement, and does all in his power to keep him in ignorance, that he may the better suit his selfish purpose, "wondering what such an one as he should want with learning" If he could be helped forward, I have no doubt he would make great progress, for he is remarkably bright, but he has not strength of himself to reach the rich subsoil

Father. This is the easiest of all the disorders above enumerated to cure, it is only to dig deep into the surface-soil some good compost and lime, repeating it after a time, when it will soon be found to strengthen the roots, so as to enable them to strike deep enough to reach the rich subsoil, and so to help themselves We will look after George Hastings, remember, I dare say we can assist him, until he is able to help himself

No 8 The sour and stubborn soil A wretched bed indeed! nothing but discontent and disorder can spring from it. The tree that is planted in such a soil, exhibits almost all the disorders that *trees are heir to* The rough and knotted bark, the faded leaf, the late springing and early falling of which show the malady contained in its system—the crooked branches and very short shoots of a whole summer's growth, while the canker-worm is ever grinding his way between the bark and the body of the tree, destroying its energies and crippling all its exertions!

I suppose you will not be at a loss to find a poor unfortunate neighbour, who is too much in the state of this pitiable tree

Frank I cannot be mistaken, it is poor Farmer Grabb! and see, here he comes—that's remarkably odd!—and how strangely he looks

Father It is so, but strange as he is, and deficient in energy and perseverance, he is greatly to be pitied, as well as blamed, for the world appears to him a blank, or even worse, the errors of his education too, haunt him, and he is always foreseeing coming events of the most gloomy character, poor man, all goes wrong with him, because he takes things by the wrong end Good day, neighbour, this is fine weather, isn't it?

Grabb Ah, 'tis all very pretty while it lasts, but I see very plainly that a change is coming, for the old rooster, when he crowed this morning, turned his tail to the rainy quarter, and that's a pretty sure sign with me, that we shall have it again before long, I never knew too much fine weather at this time of year, and I dare say I shall not be *so lucky* as to be disappointed in my expectations now, indeed I looked for rain before this, or I should have dragged down my fallow as you have yours to-day, you know the song says, "sunshine's succeeded by rain," and so I am sure it has always been with me through life, and so I have no doubt it will continue If I want sun, it rains, and when I want rain, the sun will shine in spite of me—it s enough to sour a crab. But here comes Farmer Sykes How do, neighbour?

Sykes Why, thank you, neighbour Grabb, well

and happy   My friend here and I have worked down our fallows to-day, and I am now come to invite him to join me in a work of charity, in going over to the Widow Williams's to-morrow morning, to assist her in this her time of need   But why didn't you drag your fallow to-day ? it would have worked finely, I fear you will not be ready for sowing turnips, as this is only your first ploughing, you know

Grabb   I do know it, and was always sure I should be behindhand, but, you see, I thought we should have rain to-day, and was afraid to begin, lest I should be caught in the midst of the work, I wish now that I had done as you have, for nothing would give me more pleasure than to accompany you to-morrow—hang it, I think I will do so, too

Sykes   No, you cannot, for you owe a duty to yourself and family, and until that is performed, you have no right to share in the "luxury of doing good" Charity begins at home, remember, and so you must drag down your fallow to-morrow   How I enjoy those two verses which we sing every night before going to bed ! the feeling is heavenly !

"Oh ! sweeter than the fragrant flower
At evening's dewy close,
The will, united with the power,
To succour human woes !

"And softer than the softest strain
Of music to the ear,
That placid joy we give and gain
By gratitude sincere "

Grabb   Ah, times goes gaily with you ! I'm sure I never feel in the humour to sing, either at night or morning—mine's a very different *feeling*   I often says, I was born to be unfortunate, and I have no doubt on't.   God knows my heart ; and as I says to my wife, here am I, with the best intentions in the world—but I must go, for I dare say I am wanted in twenty places at once by this time .

Sykes   Yes, there is one that wants you, I know—that confounded old rooster of yours—there he stands, with his tail in the wind, crowing away like mad

Grabb   Does he though ?   then I'll be bound we shall have it to-night after all, for he is pretty generally not far out in his reckoning, so good bye

Sykes   Poor Grabb ! he's a kind-hearted man truly, but if his father had not lived before him, and left him at his death the fine farm which he so miserably manages, he would by this time have been in the almshouse   It is pity, however, that he did not do a little in the way of cultivating his son's *mind* at the same time, his *subsoil* must be in a wretched state, I guess   Well then, neighbour, my team shall be here by peep of day to-morrow, to join yours, and as I wish to drag and roll and harrow three times in a place, the field designed for turnips, we must make up our minds to stretch a point, and complete it before we leave, and they can then collect the weeds and burn them the next day   My heart aches when I look at the poor widow of our excellent friend and her bereaved little ones, and I have made up my mind and my vow, if God spares me, to assist her in her trouble, until her fine lad is capable of taking a

14

father's place, and to work for his poor mother and sisters

Father My noble friend, I must partake with you in that luxury, and I shall not only be ready and willing, but be glad to meet you at any time with heart and hand God bless you!—good bye

Frank What a contrast! I think, however, that there must be a difference in the nature of the *tree* as well as the soil, the fruit is so very unlike

Father No doubt there is, but cultivation will always work wonders.

Frank How droll, to hear Grabb talk of a song! it must be a gloomy one to fit his state of mind, I should like to hear it

Father And so it is—words and tune, it is one of Dibdin's happiest efforts, and you must fancy it sung in the most doleful strain, to a tune in the minor key

> We bipeds made up of frail clay,
>   Alas! are the children of sorrow,
> And though brisk and merry to-day,
>   We all may be wretched to-morrow!
> For sunshine's succeeded by rain—
>   Then, fearful of life's stormy weather,
> Since pleasure can only bring pain—
>   Let us all be unhappy together!

Frank Capital!—but how would you reclaim a soil so sour, cold, and sterile, and which produces such crabbed fruit, as that of which Grabb is the similitude?

Father Oh, nothing is easier, or would be more agreeable, I would remove the soil from about the

roots to a good depth and distance, and fill the opening with fresh mould, mixed with a copious supply of lime, prune very close, and leave the event, trusting to the "sweetening influence," so beautifully expressed by the Methodist preacher—"lime to a sour, stubborn soil, is like the grace of God to a wicked man's heart"

Frank I should like to try the effect of such liming in Grabb's case, for, poor fellow, he is so miserable, that I consider him as great an object of charity and commiseration as Mrs Williams and her poor family is there nothing that can be done for him?

Father I fear not

Frank. And yet you said, cultivation will always work wonders

Father That's good, and so it will, and suppose that I get Sykes to assist us to take him up and carry him, as though he were a *bereaved widow?*

Frank Oh, pray do—I will be answerable for him At present he appears quite friendless and miserable within doors as well as without, as he says

Father. No 9 The rich and healthy surface, and poisonous subsoil This is an interesting case—shall we take the beautiful Newington peach tree, which flourished so finely for two years in our garden, and died so prematurely last year? I think we shall find the analogy complete. That fine tree was trained with the greatest care in the nursery, until it was fit for transplanting into the garden, where the soil, a fine, rich, hazel loam, was trenched and cleaned and

limed, preparatory for its reception The first season
after its removal, it bore much very fine fruit, of the
most delicious flavour, and large, handsome appearance, bringing it all to maturity, and perfectly ripen-
ing its wood The next season it bore most abundantly, and made noble shoots, which required no
pruning or heading back , its blossoms were remarkably large and of healthy appearance both fruit
and wood were well ripened, and fully testified the
care and attention which had been exercised in its
culture from the first On the appearance of the
blossoms the next spring, they were observed to be
much smaller, and paler in colour , and although the
fruit set well, many fell off when they were the size
of peas , and at midsummer many of the under
leaves withered, and fell from the branches Before
Michaelmas, the colour of the foliage had completely
changed , the fruit ceased to grow, and the tree was
declared to be infected with the disorder called the
yellows The worms had made sad havoc beneath
the bark near the ground, nor was it a matter of surprise when, on the opening of the last spring, not a
bud or blossom made their appearance—the tree was
quite dead On removing it, I was determined, if
possible, to learn the cause of such premature decay
and sudden death, and, therefore, very carefully
removed the earth from about the roots, laying them
quite bare, without wounding them All appeared
healthy, and the soil in the finest condition imaginable At length I discovered that a small and slender
root had extended itself, until it had reached a small
oozing of water, the colour of the rust of iron, which

proved to be the head of a mineral spring of the
strongest quality This small root was decayed for
a considerable way towards the body of the tree, at
least three feet from the source of the evil , and this
was, no doubt, the cause of the disease and death of
the finest tree I ever saw

Frank How very strange, that so trifling a circumstance as the point of a small root reaching a
little water at such a distance from the tree, should
be the cause of such sudden destruction!

Father It is—but to show you how certainly this
was the cause, I will copy from our favourite Tull
an account of some experiments which he made expressly with the view of proving the truth of the
position, that vegetables will take up and circulate,
indiscriminately, the most deleterious, as well as the
most wholesome substances, and that this they often
do to their destruction.

"Exp. 1 I put a mint stalk into a glass of water,
but I immersed one string of its roots, being brought
over the top of that glass, into another glass of salt
water contiguous to the top of the other glass—this
mint died very soon

"Exp. 2 I put the upper root of another mint into
a small glass of ink—this plant was also killed by
some of the ink ingredients

"Exp 3. I made a very strong liquor with water
and the bruised seed of the garlic, and placed the
top of it close to the top of another glass, having in
it a mint plant, two or three of whose upper roots, put
into this stinking liquor, and there remaining, it killed
the mint in some time . and when the edges of the

14*

leaves of the mint began to change colour, I chewed many of them in my mouth, and found at first the strong flavour of the mint, but that was soon over, and then *the nauseous taste of the garlic was soon perceptible "*

So you see how readily plants, whose roots reach a poisonous subsoil, imbibe and circulate to their destruction the deleterious matter I once grew some turnips on land having a wet subsoil, and on storing them for winter use, I observed that the point of the tap root of every one was decayed, but as that was not near the bulb, I did not consider the circumstance of any consequence: on opening the pit in the winter, however, I found that three parts of them were rotten, and the stench arising from these had infected the remainder, so that the cattle refused to eat them

Frank How satisfactorily have you accounted for the decay and death of our favourite tree! what a pity that you could not have ascertained the cause during its lifetime, as it might so easily have been prevented, merely by separating that small root from the body of the tree!

Father Truly, but the lesson has not been lost upon us, for you know that I have recovered many trees that have been infected by the yellows and the worms, by trenching and dressing the land with lime, and by removing the bad soil from amongst the roots

And now, do you know any young and promising individual, whose untimely death might be likened to the decay and death of our favourite tree?

Frank Yes Henry Templeton

Father Exactly Of an excellent and highly respected family, he was the brightest hope—an only

son With a mind and body cast in beauty's mould, he was the " observed of all observers ," even in the nursery his education had commenced, and the wisdom displayed by his amiable parents in this particular, was crowned with perfect success His youth was spent in acquiring knowledge of the most useful and valuable kinds, and the commencement of his public life—which might be compared to the planting out our tree from the nursery—was hailed by his friends with the brightest expectations We well know the esteem and respect which he won from all who knew him, while his gentle and amiable and refined manners were the admiration of every one I remember the time when he commenced the study of the law under Counsellor S——, and how fortunate his family considered him, in the choice of his fellow-student, Charles E——, as his particular friend Alas! that very circumstance proved the total ruin of him and the hopes of his family, for Charles E—— was a young man addicted to every species of vice and wickedness, and possessed of the most consummate hypocrisy! On one fatal evening he prevailed upon Henry to accompany him to the gaming-table, and his destruction was sealed In a short year from this time he returned to his father's house, an emaciated being—his health destroyed, his mind frenzied, and in the last stage of consumption— only to sigh out his soul in penitence, in the arms of his broken-hearted parents and sisters! Poor Henry Templeton! one small root, penetrating to the poison in the subsoil, was the cause of indescribable suffering, misery, remorse, anguish, and death to himself, and distress unspeakable to his tenderly attached family, and a numerous circle of young and much-loved friends!

Frank Poor Henry Templeton! who would have thought that we could find so true a portrait of him, in our beautiful and unfortunate peach tree!

Father But here is one more soil for examination No 10 It is, to appearance, a happy mixture, and in the highest state of cultivation, but the tree which is planted in it, makes no progress It is not diseased, but can scarcely be called healthy, it blossoms in season, but seems not to possess energy sufficient to bring its fruit to perfection, and although when produced it is fair to the eye, it has little flavour and soon perishes Its shoots are not deformed, nor do they require much pruning, but the foliage has a weak and delicate appearance, although it cannot be denominated sickly Its bark is thin and clean, and its foliage does not fall or change colour prematurely, but it makes no progress—there is no strength in its growth, and yet there is no sensible defect—an ornamental tree, but of very little value, although of the choicest fruit-bearing species

Frank Why, what can be the matter with the tree then?

Father Nothing—the *matter* is in the soil, which has been too highly manured, and made light and porous by such frequent dressings—in fact, this tree might be compared to a rich, indolent, unemployed young man, eaten up with *ennui!* no disease, but no health—no pain, but no pleasure—with energy sufficient to put forth a blossom, but not enough to bring

it to perfection—no fear of dying, but no hope in living—blameless, but praiseless—does no harm, nor any good—and may as well be dead as alive

Frank Well, I would not be a gentleman if I could But how would you set about curing such a nameless disease?

Father I *would try it with affliction* I would open the ground about the root, amputate some of them, and mix clay and lime with fresh strong loam, for filling in, and then I would prune close and hard, shrouding the branches pretty close to the stem of the tree, and await the result with confidence.

Frank Well, those would be *hard lines*, as Grabb says

Father Yes, but I have known many such characters, who have had abundant cause to exclaim "it is good for me that I have been afflicted" You know there is the son of old Judge Thomson, who, while his wealth remained with him, has often complained of the trouble of eating, and could not bear the idea of walking abroad, even on the score of health, was charitably disposed, but could not prevail upon himself to use the least exertion, even were it to save a fellow-creature from starving—it is even said that, when in a passion with his servants, he has declared that he would kick them, if it were not so much trouble! But the fire which destroyed his wealth, purified and sanctified his soul, he is now happy, because he is industrious, cheerful, because usefully employed, and finds it no painful exertion to walk miles, to render service to a suffering neighbour he is now rich in good works and sound bodily health, and often exclaims, in the fulness of his heart "it is good for me that I have been afflicted !" Let us close by reading Dr Drennan's beautiful hymn, "The Fruits of Benevolence"

> The husbandman goes forth a-field
> What hopes his heart expand '
> What calm delight his labours yield '
> A harvest from his hand
>
> The nobler husbandry of mind
> And culture of the heart—
> Shall such with men less favour find ?
> Less genuine joy impart ?
>
> Ah ' no—your goodness strikes a root
> That dies not, nor decays ,
> And future life shall yield the fruit,
> That blossoms now in praise
>
> The youthful hopes, which now expand
> Their green and tender leaves,
> Shall spread a plenty o'er the land,
> In rich and yellow sheaves
>
> Thus a small bounty, well bestowed,
> May perfect heaven s high plan ,
> First daughter to the love of God,
> Is charity to man '
>
> 'Tis he, who scatters blessings round,
> Adores his Maker best ,
> His walk through life is mercy-crowned,
> His bed of death is blest

DIALOGUE XV

PLOUGHING

Father. Take care, Frank, how you lead the horse over this ice ; do you see the water flowing underneath it ? This brings to our recollection the wise ordination of Providence in the freezing of water, which is in direct opposition to almost every other known law of nature All other bodies grow heavier while cooling but if this were the case with water, the ice would, as soon as formed on the surface, sink to the bottom of the rivers, when, the surface again freezing and again sinking, it would soon choke up their beds, and the water, still flowing over and freezing, would cause a deluge of ice over the surface of the earth of incalculable thickness, to the inevitable destruction of every living thing, man not excepted The reason of its being lighter in a state of ice than water—which is, you know, the cause of its swimming—is, it contains a great quantity of air, as you might see, by those bubbles which are formed in it, and this air is *ordained* to be the cause of its breaking up at the time of thawing , but for this, a mountain of ice would be the work of a summer for the sun to penetrate and dissolve , and as I told you the expansion of ice at the time of freezing is extremely great, bursting with ease the most solid bodies, so also, the air which is contained in these bubbles, when expanded by warmth is equally irresistible, and in very cold countries, the explosions which take place, occasioned by this expansion, at the time of the breaking up of frost, are dreadful, equal to the loudest thunder! So thus it is—water contracts in bulk as it cools, until it has reached the freezing point, when, immediately, its nature becomes changed, and it then grows lighter and of larger bulk, as it freezes

Frank. What a wonderful contrivance! I perfectly understand how that, if ice were to sink in water, it would soon stop the course of rivers, for one of the little streams in the meadow has become frozen to the bottom, and the consequence is, the flowing over of the water, and this again freezing, and the water again flowing and again freezing, there is a sheet of ice twenty yards in width.

I hope, however, the frost will soon break up, for I see that our new plough is just brought home, and I long to try it, its fine wide share and long mould-plate must make great havoc amongst the weeds I have often been astonished at the variety of ploughs that have been invented, each professing to be superior to every other. Is it not possible to determine which is the *best*, that so a preference might be given to it above all others? There is not only a difference in the formation of the body and mould-plate, but also in the mode of working them, some are with two wheels, others with one, some with a foot, and others with neither now which is to be preferred, or is there, after all, no essential difference?

Father A very interesting question, and that we may thoroughly understand the subject, we will go into its examination when we come to use our new plough in turning the two acre field for sugar beet,

which was, you know, ploughed very deep in November of last year, preparatory to a spring working, then you will perceive the advantage of practice, when compared with mere theory, and will be enabled to decide which is, upon the whole, best suited for the purpose of *cultivating the soil*, that is the question with us, with many others it is, I believe, *which follows the horses most easily*

Frank I have often heard, that the plough which follows the horses the easiest, must be the best, now there might be a great difference in this respect, but as the horses cannot tell any thing about it, how are we to judge?

Father An instrument has been invented to fix to the end of the beam of the plough by which the horses are made to draw, it is called an *Eodometer*, and has an index, by which may be seen, very exactly, how much power is required to draw it when put to different depths it is something like the little instrument with which your mother weighs articles in the house

Frank I know, it draws out in length in proportion to the weight which is attached to it, and the number of pounds weight is stamped on the little index rod This is a very clever contrivance, and must decide the question in an instant, for that plough must certainly be the best which requires the least power to drag it, provided the depth be the same, and I wonder why this best plough has not got into general use, to the exclusion of all others

Father How easily you have decided the question, and in the way too, in which many other interesting

15

questions are decided, namely, by mere theory, by taking a statement for granted, and acting upon it but if the statement be fallacious, so must be the conclusions which are drawn from it, just as if a man were to take for granted that the foundations of a house are good, and build upon them without examination, they might be defective, and if they are, so will be the house, when completed, although it might look fair to the eye.

Frank How well I understand that, I see now that there might be other considerations connected with the subject, and I long for an opportunity to decide by practice

Father And as I consider it a question of the greatest consequence, we will lose no time in making *the experiment*, on the breaking up of the frost

———

Frank. Well, father, here is a fine day, and we are quite ready, which plough shall we commence with?

Father Put the horses to the single-wheel patent plough, invented by a person named *Plenty*, which is in very general use in many of the counties in England. Do you know the meaning of the term *patent*?

Frank Perhaps not, exactly

Father The inventor of this plough thinks so well of its merits, that he has asked of the government to secure to himself the making of them for a certain number of years, and the government issues an order that no other person shall presume to make them for a time agreed upon, under a severe penalty, this is

granting a patent, which in England costs about one hundred pounds sterling (five hundred dollars) But now for our ploughing match !

> The weather fine, the season now,
> Drive on, my boy, " God speed the plough "

Well, Frank, what think you?

Frank. I shall be careful how I say again what I think It appears, however, to be a heavy instrument with which to turn a furrow eight inches wide and five inches deep, which is as much as it will do, to be sure it goes straight, and makes what is called good work, but after all, it does not turn the land *over*, it merely sets it on edge, or a little more, and passes on

Father But now for your criterion of a good plough, do you not think it follows the horses easily?

Frank I now understand why you said, the object with us ought to be, to ascertain which is the plough best suited for the purpose of cultivating the soil, and that you thought this was not the object with some, those for instance, who are more careful of the shining coats of their horses, than with the proper stirring of the soil

Father As there is so little resistance against the mould-plate, in consequence of the small furrow which we are compelled to carry, and the manner in which it leaves it, setting it on edge, or nearly so, and not turning it over, I am inclined to believe that to this circumstance is to be attributed, a part at least of its good name to be sure, the length of the beam and handles gives great facility for guiding it straight and steadily, but do you remark the very narrow furrow which it leaves, in which the furrow-horse has to walk, and how he treads down the land-side of it with two of his feet, because there is not room for him to walk in the furrow? neither is there room for the furrow-slice when it is turned, for it lies so nearly on edge as to leave a seam or channel, from whence the weeds will spring with redoubled vigour, if the land is left even for a short time, un-ploughed This plough is altogether unfit for the use of those who have an interest in the soil, and the unlevel state in which it leaves the bottom of the furrow, in some places called *raftering*, is decisive proof of its inefficiency

We will now try the short and light American plough, but are you aware that the swing plough is managed in direct opposition to that with one or two wheels? for, if I wish to go deeper, I *lift up* the handles, whilst to cause the plough with wheels to take a deeper furrow, it is necessary to *press them down*

Frank I was just remarking that you appear some-times to press upon the handles, which I have often heard you say is improper, as it makes nearly a horse draft difference in the working of a plough, and that, I suppose, cannot be good, at any rate, indeed, I never see you do so while using a plough with a wheel

Father As there is no wheel on which the beam can rest, the plough is liable to drop a little when the land is soft or wet, and this sends the point of the

share so deep into the earth, that unless I were to raise it by pressing upon the handles, the plough would sink so deep that the utmost exertion of the horses would not be sufficient to move it On the other hand, if the land is hard or stony, it is neces-sary to lift up the handles to send the point deeper into the soil, and with those ploughs that are short and light, *so high*, that the mould-plate is often raised so much, as to be out of its proper position for turning the furrow properly over And hence it is, that land which has been turned with such a plough, is often found to be less level, and to be full of *baulks*, or parts that are left unploughed, than that which has been worked with a wheel plough This constant ten-dency to rise and sink, is exceedingly troublesome to the ploughman, and distressing to the horses, for they are liable to be galled by the collar, do you see how tenderly they seem to advance in this hard spot, and how the traces shake and jar them?

Frank Yes I do, and now that I take the trace in my hand, I feel it too

Father Nothing could be better adapted to the purpose for which these short and light ploughs were designed, with a short beam and handles, as well as a short bed or waist, they were admirably fitted for turning the earth amongst stumps and stones and roots on fresh-cleared lands, where, in the hands of an expert ploughman, it takes place of spade, mattock, and pickaxe, spuddling the earth from amongst them with the greatest ingenuity, but in cleared land, where to go a *leetle* deeper and to turn the furrow well up and over, is the soul of good

15*

tillage, they are altogether unsuitable , for, in consequence of their lightness and shortness they offer no resistance to a thick furrow-slice, but, like an unfaithful servant, are always slipping out of their work, leaving it half done   The apology which is sometimes offered, that you can plough nearer the ends and leave a narrow headland, is the most futile that can be conceived, for the headlands should be wide and well defined, thrown up high and round, with the furrow at the head of the ridges, wide and deep, serving the purpose of a water furrow, to receive and carry off the drainings of the ridges in wet weather   The shortness of the body of this plough is the cause of its rising and falling so abruptly and so readily, fitting it peculiarly for its working amongst stumps, but for the same reason, unfitting it for every other purpose , they are excellent therefore, but not for general use

Now, we will try our new plough, which is perhaps, the most perfect for many purposes that can well be imagined   It is either a swing or a wheel plough, but in nine cases out of ten, the wheel can be dispensed with, its length and weight being sufficient to keep it at the depth required, provided the rack at the head is properly adjusted   the objection to its weight is groundless, for in very light land, that is of no importance, and in a heavy soil, it is necessary to form proper resistance to a thick and heavy furrow-slice, for here, a light plough would *rise up and walk off*   While, therefore, the length of the body of this plough keeps it steady to its work, every little obstacle is apt to throw a light plough out of it,

and its constant tendency to rise, compels the ploughman, as has already been observed, to raise the handles so high to counteract it, as either to lift it out of the ground altogether, or to send the point so deep as to require an immediate and sudden reversion by pressing upon the handles—thus it is ever on the poise, like a pair of scales, demanding of the ploughman incessant care and labour, and performing badly at last

Frank How finely the noble mould-plate turns the furrow-slice over, burying the weeds, so that there is not one remaining on the surface, and breaking up the land, so as scarcely to require harrowing

Father True—but this very excellent quality shows that it is not well adapted to the purpose of cutting across weedy fallows preparatory to harrowing or dragging , in that operation, the furrow-slice ought not to be turned so completely over, for if it is, the harrow cannot act upon so level a surface, so as to drag over the clods to be crushed by the roller , the furrow should in this case be set more on edge, but that, you see, cannot be done by this plough , it requires one of a different form, with less curve in the mould-plate   Still, however, every plough should throw out a furrow wide enough to permit the furrow-horse to walk in it with ease, and without which it is not possible to plough clean

Frank Yes, I have always heard you say, he is not a good gardener who does not keep a good, wide, open trench in digging , and I can now understand the advantage of a wide and clean furrow in ploughing

Father Nor is the plough which we are now using, suitable for hard or stony land, its wide wing prevents its entering a hard soil, and during a hot and dry season it would be useless for a considerable portion of the summer, nor is it for this and some other reasons, the best for turning lay land preparatory for immediate sowing on such land the furrow should be narrow, but with a wing so wide, it would not be possible to carry a narrow furrow, so as to place it in a proper position for seeding A person in England* has invented a plough, which for this work is perhaps superior to all others, it is furnished with three spare shares of different widths, the narrowest being used for this purpose, and it is said a man has turned a furrow of two hundred and fifty yards in length so straight, that, by placing the head in it, a person might see from one end to the other, without any obstruction By some peculiar process at the time of casting, the points and wings of these shares are case-hardened on their *underside*, so that they point and sharpen themselves, the upper surface being soft, wears away by working, leaving the under part sharp as a knife! It is said, they are cast on a bed of sand, sprinkled over with powdered charcoal, which converts the part coming in contact with it, into steel With a narrow share, this plough will penetrate a hard soil, when no other that I have ever seen, would even *look at it*, but its great length of waist, with its long beam and handles, fit it for turning up a *turnpike* It has the quality too, of turning completely the furrow-slice, leaving it impenetra-

* Jefferis, of London

ble to the harrow—it is therefore unsuitable for fallowing land that is full of root-weeds

So that we ought not to expect to find any one plough with the different qualities of all combined but every intelligent and industrious man should keep a set of ploughs for various purposes It is the most important of all implements, and is deserving our most serious regard, but let it be repeated, there is one qualification which is necessary in all, at all times, and in all places, namely, that a furrow shall be left sufficiently wide for the horse to walk in, and to receive the next furrow-slice, be that intended to lie at an angle of forty-five degrees or at any other

Frank At an angle of forty-five degrees! pray what is that? and how am I to know when it lies at an angle of forty-five degrees?

Father I will show you the circumference of a globe, let the size be large or small, is denominated three hundred and sixty degrees Now, if we cut a circle of paper and call the circumference three hundred and sixty degrees by folding in half, there will then be just half the number of degrees remaining, namely, one hundred and eighty, if we fold this again, we shall find the number of degrees remaining to be ninety another folding will give us a wedge-shaped piece of paper, which, if it be placed on one of its straight sides on a flat surface, will show you exactly what is an angle of forty-five degrees, if you cast your eye along the upper straight edge, beginning at the point

Frank I understand this exactly

Father One very serious objection to the general

mode of ploughing in this country, arises from the
hurry with which this most important of all operations is performed, it is a cause of boasting, to be
able to turn an acre of land in the shortest possible
time, without, I fear, any regard to the manner in
which it is done, to this haste is to be, in great part,
attributed the irregularities observable at the beginning of the furrows in almost every field we witness,
occasioned by the too sudden elevation or depression
of a plough of light and short construction, and a desire to make the headlands as narrow as possible,
and I have never seen a ploughman turn about to
take up that portion of land which has thus been
missed—as is always done when proper time and
attention are paid to the work—trusting to the next
turn, when he might take a deeper and larger furrow,
and with it cover the defect, thus leaving a solid portion of the earth underneath a furrow that lies too
high, but which he thinks might be levelled by cross-
harrowing I once knew a faithless servant of this
sort, who got *served out* in a very unexpected way
while practising this sleight of hand his employer
had witnessed what he had been doing from the other
side of the fence, and on hearing the fellow exclaim
as he passed one of these *baulks,* " that's covered,"
sprang over, and hitting him over the head with his
stick, by which his hat was knocked off, picked it
up, and clapping it on for him, exclaimed also, " and
that's covered !"

But a cause for this hurry in ploughing, might
sometimes be traced to the weakness of the horses,
who, unless it be done by a sudden exertion of their

whole strength, are not able to bear a protracted and
steady strain, competent to the task in none of the
operations on a farm is it so necessary to have sufficient team-power as in ploughing, with a weak
team, not even the best ploughman can make good
work, nor can land be stirred to a sufficient depth to
bring a crop to maturity It might not, perhaps, be
too much to say, many crops depend as much for
support on the subsoil as on the surface, especially in
a time of drought, and it is becoming at length to
be understood, *that very deep ploughing* is essential to
the perfection of the crop

Frank And yet I have often heard you laugh at
the directions which we so often find in books for
the necessity of very deep ploughing, without, as
you observe, the writers being by possibility able to
judge of the actual depth of the staple of the surface-
soil, and when, for aught they know, three inches might
be too deep, while again, as many feet in some soils
might be turned with advantage Now how is this ?

Father An excellent observation, and it shows that
your mind is awake But, after hearing me say, the
proper depth must be governed by the staple of the
surface-soil, and that every farmer knows if the sterile
subsoil be turned up, it will be to the ruin of the land,
what will you think when I now say, all land should
be ploughed deep, without regard to the depth of the
surface-soil ?

Frank What, so deep as to turn up the sterile subsoil ?

Father Yes, to the depth, if you please, of two or
three inches of the sterile and poisonous subsoil

Frank Well, I don't know what I should *say*, and I should not like to *think* much about what is so directly opposed to all our experience, and all that we have always thought and said

Father Well, let us see what we can make of it All good farmers in this and in every other country, will one day plough up every acre of their uncropped and arable land before winter, as is the custom in the best-farmed districts in England This system will apply to every country, be its soil, climate, and circumstances what they may I know many large farms in that country, where it is the custom to make the Christmas cheer depend on the due and seasonable performance of this necessary part of their routine, which, if not fulfilled at that time, there is no treat. Now, at that season of the year, and particularly in this country, where the soil has not generally been stirred to the necessary depth to sustain the crops in a dry season, I would recommend *very deep ploughing*, in large and straight furrows, and as unbroken as possible, turning up the subsoil to a depth which to an unpractised eye would have the appearance of *dead ruin!* leaving open water-furrows and well defined headlands, so to lie until the season of spring tillage, for the purpose of being thoroughly pulverized by the winter's frost and rain, which would be about as good as a covering of manure In the spring then, these furrows must be taken up by the plough, and be very carefully returned, unbroken, to the place from whence they were taken, after which, the surface, in fine order for working, may be ploughed and properly cultivated for the re-

ception of the seed, being extremely careful, however, not to go so deep as to touch the returned subsoil, which will thus be in fine order to receive the tap-roots of the crop, having received a deep stirring and melioration from atmospheric exposure, of incalculable benefit to whatever crop might be planted on the land I conceive that the office of the *tap-roots* of plants is, to send up moisture from the subsoil, and during the great heats of summer, I have no doubt a large portion of their support arises from this source, while their *lateral roots*, which are very differently constructed from their tap-roots, are busily engaged in providing them *food*, by pushing their ramifications in all directions, like net-work, in the surface-soil

Frank Well, I can now tell you what I would *say*—that I should suppose this plan would be the best and most beneficial that could be adopted—far better than the stirring of the subsoil at the bottom of the furrows by the grub-plough so much recommended, as the subsoil is in this case not only loosened, but absolutely enriched by exposure during the whole winter to the frosts and snows and rains, while the still deeper and untouched subsoil must imbibe much benefit by coming in contact with the rich surface-soil, and the decomposition of the herbage that might have been growing on it at the time of turning it down in the autumn I declare, I have no doubt the benefit to be derived from this management, would in many cases be equal to the rent of the land, and obtained too at the cost of one ploughing!

Father Capitally argued! Now what do you

16

think of our mode of distinguishing between the offices of the tap and the lateral roots of plants—the one providing them with drink and the other with food?

Frank It appears very interesting—but may plants, such as wheat and many others, which do not seem to be furnished with tap-roots, be supposed to subsist without drink?

Father On examination, you will find that all plants are furnished with what might be termed tap-roots, easily distinguishable from those which are denominated *lateral*, and that the carrot, although peculiarly tap-rooted, is yet furnished with lateral roots, which will be found pushing into the surface-soil in all directions, while the lowermost part of the root will, upon inspection, appear of quite a different formation from those

Frank Now then, I see the importance of deep ploughing, and can understand why it is, that while our neighbours are complaining of their crops turning blue, and becoming curled and affected with all sorts of diseases, ours go on and come to such perfection, as to induce the farmers about us to apply to us for *change of seed*, while you never find it necessary to do any thing of the kind

Father This may be called a practical lecture on ploughing, delivered at the handles of the plough—in my estimation the best lecture-room

Now let us see, by our "Farmer's Pocket Companion," how much land we have ploughed to-day, I will step it off, and do you then turn to the book—there, just 82 yards long, and 60 yards wide, now, at page 38 you will find the account ready cast up.

Frank I have it in an instant, 1 acre and 3 perches Well, this is the most valuable "Companion" that a farmer can have, why, I can by it find the content, in measurement, of any field on our farm in a few minutes, as also the weight of any crop by measuring off a small space, the quantity of seed sown per acre, the quantity of land necessary to form an acre, while the tables at the end treat of so many things, planting, manuring, ploughing, &c How I wonder that every farmer in the country does not get it! Where did you buy it?

Father I have used it for many years, and would not be without it for ten times its cost, it will be published immediately in Philadelphia, where it may then be obtained at a very moderate price, and will no doubt be in the hands of almost every practical man in the United States And now, as it appears by it that we have ploughed an acre of land in our day's work, we will quit I consider that *quantity*, under ordinary circumstances, sufficient for that time, the *quality* of the work being taken into the account.

DIALOGUE XVI

MID-WINTER

Frank Oh! father, what a dreadful night! The wind blows a hurricane, and the snow comes down in whirlwinds! I fear our beautiful fruit trees will suffer very much, for I have heard their branches break with the weight of snow which is frozen upon them, this is mid-winter truly! How I pity our poor neighbours, who are unprepared for this trying season; many of them are, I know, very scantily provided, and to them the roaring of the elements must be frightful As I passed Farmer Bowen's this evening, with the heifers from the lower pasture, I saw his poor wife screwing the pieces of old garments tighter into the broken windows, and poor John, shovelling the snow from a few logs, that he might take them into the house for their evening's fire, while the wretched cattle were creeping around the fences for shelter, moaning so piteously, and the dog, who was chained, was howling so frightfully, for the snow was beating full into the house upon him, but *poorer* than all, and more to be pitied, was the farmer himself, who, with both hands thrust down into his pockets, his teeth hard clenched, and his face drawn into wrinkles, was crouching behind the old pear tree, with his eyes fixed upon the warring of the elements, the picture of despair! Oh, it was a perfect scene of desolation!

Father It must have been a heart-rending sight But you know I have often told neighbour Bowen how it would be with him, and when I saw him wasting his time in the summer, and caring so little for the future, I could not help expressing myself strongly, which is the cause, you know, of the coolness that is between us If the winter should prove such as we have reason to expect, from its early and violent commencement, he and his poor cattle must starve, for I know that he has made but little provision either for them or himself. Poor man, he must think, as Grabb says, that the pleasures and indepen-

dence of a farmer's life are all a *hum*, and it is a serious fact, that a farmer's life, unless he take time by the forelock and be even with the seasons, is of all lives the most miserable, for the short days and long nights of winter in the country, have but little to cheer them, unless there is *sunshine within*, and to be met at every turn, with the dull and black and reproachful countenances of every creature about you, hungry, cold, houseless, and wretched, oh! I know of nothing so forlorn and wo-begone On the other hand, to us who enjoy the pleasure of witnessing, on such a night as the present, our horses and cattle comfortably housed and well fed, with plenty of food and fuel for ourselves, no employment would seem to offer such a source of real happiness What, for instance, can equal the pleasure of visiting our stables before going to bed, on such a night as this, to hear the cows chewing the cud, while lying on their warm beds of clean straw, and the horses grinding their hay in such exact time and *tune*—for the grinding apparatus of each horse has, you know, its own peculiar key-note—I do declare I know of no music more sweet And I once had a friend, an old farmer, who passed an hour in the stable every night after supper, to enjoy it, declaring there was no *playhouse* music to be compared with it!

Frank And I too have enjoyed it, and it is, as you say, on such a night as this, peculiarly sweet

Father This, however, is a luxury which those only who have *sunshine within* can enjoy, according to that most beautiful song—

16*

Sigh not for summer flowers '—
What, though the dark sky lowers ?
Welcome, ye wintry hours '
Our sunshine is within
Though, to the west retreating,
Daylight so soon is fleeting,
Now, happy friends are meeting,
And now our joys begin
    Sigh not for summer flowers

Round us 'tis deeply snowing,
Hark ! the loud tempest blowing '
See the dark torrent flowing—
How wild the skies appear'
But, can the whirlwind move us ?
No ' with this roof above us,
Near to the friends that love us,
We still have sunshine here '
    Sigh not for summer flowers

Frank. That is beautiful indeed But, father, I have sometimes thought, that the difference which there is between such *good* and such *bad* management, must arise, in part, from the systems pursued, and which might therefore be denominated the old and the new systems , for, until latterly, it was the custom with many, and still is I believe with some, to farm with as little expense as possible, supposing that the business of agriculture would not pay for good management

Father Well, I believe there is truth in the observation, for I have known some who have changed their plan of *cheap farming*, and confess, that they are gainers by it, in many ways, and chiefly, in reaping more profit and enjoying more pleasure

Frank And, I suppose, these considerations ought to be reckoned worth something

Father Certainly , the last not least When I visited my friend Starkey, in ——— county the last autumn, I was struck with the *ability* of himself and his land, which were both of the highest order , and also, at the same time, with the strange manner in which things were conducted , and all according to the custom of the country too " They do so here," was the reply, when I animadverted upon what I saw, with the freedom which one friend is apt to take with another , for instance, when I pointed out the weedy state of the crops—weedy in proportion to the natural fertility of the soil—I was answered, " but the people here find it will not pay the expense to clean them " Or, the turning in of a heavy crop of weeds in full seed, " Oh, the people here find there is no harm in that, the grain will grow and come good." Or the wretched bad ploughing, on light land, with a very short and light plough, which was oftentimes no sooner in than out of the soil , with the furrows too large and high, and sometimes too low, with baulks and correspondent hollows, large enough in which to bury a sheep, with no well-defined headlands , and a crop of couch, beyond any thing that I ever before witnessed, " Oh ! that's well enough, the harrow will make all level, and we find it will not pay to be too particular " His stock of cattle was very large; and truly delightful was it to see with what kindness every animal upon the farm was treated, a whip was not permitted to be used on any occasion And when my friend and his amiable partner would walk amongst the cows and young heifers, calling them by endearing names, and feeding them with salt, with which upon these occasions he would always provide himself, it was pleasant to see the animals run and thrust their noses into his pocket, to obtain a lick of the precious morsel, follow him all over the pasture, and into the house if they should ! All this was lovely, and spoke a language which could not be misunderstood But when I saw that the cattle were of the coarse, wiry-haired breed, of a colour and feel in the handling, that indicated any thing but milk and beef, and heard that they had been selected from amongst the most valuable stock in that part of the country, " for they would winter cheaply," I was satisfied that my excellent friend had imbibed the prejudices of the ignorant people about him, and had adopted the old system of *cheap farming* And oftentimes, when I took the liberty of representing to him the advantages of a different course of management, I was answered, " But it won't pay, my dear sir, the people here find that it won't pay." He had no stock of hay for the winter, for the people in that part of the country, found that it would not pay the expense of making ! Now, my friend, with bodily and mental powers of the highest order, with a capital, sufficient to manage a farm of unprecedented richness and fertility, and all his own, by late purchase, with an elegant partner and two lovely children, had permitted himself to be influenced in his judgment, by about as ignorant a set of men, calling themselves agriculturists, as I ever met in my life One of them said, they had tried lime, but it would not do in that part of the

country, that to plant potatoes in any other way than in hills at four feet distance, and by hand, would not answer in that part of the country, that although it might do very well to plough them *in* and plough them *out* in some other places, yet, although he had never known it tried, he knew very well that it would never answer in that part of the country ! That it was a bad plan to weed the crops, for it had been tried, and found that such management would not pay in that country But, amid plenty of land of the very highest fertility, requiring only good management to produce a return of a hundred fold, he was a strong advocate for draining the most beautiful natural fish-pond in front of my friend's house, for, he *conceited*, it would make " a most almighty meadow !" This man was a smith also, and as the shoes of my friend's horses were always dropping off, before they were half worn, I took the liberty of recommending a plan of clenching the nails, which I had known practised elsewhere, and by which they would be sure to be secured, he replied, he had never known that done, but he supposed it would not answer, for it was not the practice in that part of the country !

Frank Now that is the *old school*, and a wretched one it is ! I do not wonder that such farmers should have the character of being—and I am sure they deserve it—the most unenlightened class of the community Why, it is a downright insult, to say of any art or science, " it won't pay for good management," did any thing in the world ever pay for bad management?

Father Good, but we have known a case which will prove, that good management will pay in *any country* There is our friend Daniel Finley, who took the farm of Shields in —— county, in the midst of the most ignorant and besotted class of farmers that can be conceived of. They had already driven off two very respectable men from distant counties, by their persecutions, terrifying and threatening their servants, driving away their cattle to distant parts of the country, &c Daniel's coming amongst them was a source of merriment to them, and they nick-named him "The New School" Fortunately, he was a man of strong mind and body, with a determined will, which would have required the united strength of half a dozen of their weak teams to move him from his purpose But what was better than this, he was blest with a wife, almost unequalled in the experience of the necessary duties of a farm, and a family of six children, some of both sexes, able to assist their parents both within doors and without, he was, therefore, a host in himself On coming to the farm, as he found the neighbours would not call upon *him*, he made a point of visiting *them*; told them, candidly, he meant to manage his own concerns, that nothing would give him more pleasure than to be on good terms with them, while, to have it in his power to assist them, he should consider a real luxury, but he must be permitted to follow his own way, that was all he stipulated for At parting, he would offer them his hand, which, when they grasped—about the size, as one of them declared, of a small shoulder of mutton—and received a *grip* in

return, which made them feel it to the elbow, they perceived that such a man was not to be played with He was compelled to hire help from the neighbourhood, and on meeting these men for the first time, said, "Now, my good fellows, I am come a stranger amongst you, and I dare say you will think my ways strange also, all I expect of you is, to do exactly what I shall tell you to do, and leave the consequences to me Never care how ridiculous my plans may appear to you, 'tis I alone who must answer for them, and if you get tired of me, or I should grow tired of you, let us not be afraid to say so, and part good friends As I have the fullest confidence in my own abilities, I do not wish you to take the trouble to tell me, how they do things in this country, or even to *mention* the way in which others proceed, all I shall ever require of you is, obedience while you are with me, so God bless all our endeavours to do what is right" And on separating with them he gave each a shake by the hand, which reminded them of the squeeze *which Jack Sharp got in the horse-mill!* He was up the first in the house, and the last in bed, was always upon their backs, as they expressed it, but cheerful as a lark, and always pleasant in manners, but *very distant!* that was the secret of his management. Like the captain of the ship, who, on first coming on board said to his men, "I wish to treat you well, but look in my face, and say, if you think I am a man you can take liberties with"

In the midst of a country, where the greatest recommendation of a cow was, that she would winter cheaply, or in other words, would bear starving, he introduced a dairy that would pay for *keeping*—for shelter, and good food in the winter—and a portion of these being winter milk cows, he was enabled to supply the market with—what had never before been seen there—excellent fresh butter in winter, for which he obtained his own price And while his neighbours were killing off their sheep before winter, and disposing of them for about the value of their skins, he would stall-feed his, and have mutton in the market about Christmas, that almost made the poor farmers about him fat, even to look at

Frank. Ah, I see how all this was done, it was by good management in the summer, by preparing for such weather as that which we now experience

Father Exactly, his object was, to *keep* his stock in the winter, and make them *pay* for it and instead of boasting that he had wintered his cattle for almost nothing, and in return, to have but little besides a bag of bones for his pains, I have often heard him declare, that he would not exchange his winter dung-heap, for the whole dairy of some of his neighbours

One remarkable mode of his management was to grow large quantities of oats, and the Silesian, or white sugar beet, never to thrash any of his oats, but to cut them all up in the straw, by means of a chaff-cutter attached to his thrashing-mill, and to feed them, with plenty of the beets, to his horses, fatting cattle, cows in milk, and fatting sheep—a plan of fatting stock in the winter about as near perfection as can well be conceived of—so he never sold any oats, but almost all his corn, and fed the stalks to his

young stock His greatest care was, to provide most abundantly for all his stock during winter, and I have known him purchase capital cows of his neighbours during that season for a very small sum, as they had not the means of keeping them, and sell them to them in the spring, and instead of fatting stock in the summer, he would mow as much hay as possible, grow abundance of oats and beets, and purchase lean stock in the autumn for winter feeding, by which means he obtained better prices for his fat cattle, and, what he valued much more, mountains of dung for spring dressing—this he called the *moving principle of his machinery* He had not been on his farm a year, before the natives were astonished, and no more was heard of "the new school," but they yet stick to their old prejudices, and cannot believe that *their* farms will *ever* pay for good management, for, as the Smith said, although they never tried it, yet they are fully convinced it would never pay the expense in their part of the country, to manure and weed crops, and house cattle in the winter and feed them

Frank Then the new system is simply this—to *feed* stock in the winter, instead of *starving* it

Father. Just so, and a very short and satisfactory definition it is But to be enabled to do this, the greatest exertions must be made in summer to secure abundant resources for that season, and by cultivating the Silesian beet, we are enabled to do *what* we wish, and *all* we wish

Frank The cultivation of that root must be of the utmost importance to the stock farmer, as well as to the feeder and dairyman What astonishing accounts

17

of its produce we hear and read of! and the hold which it has obtained on public estimation it keeps, for sugar-beet beef and mutton and butter are all the rage Were you not engaged in the first introduction of that crop into this country?

Father As agent to the " Beet-Sugar Society of Philadelphia," the seed which I selected in France and sent to this country, proved to be of the purest kind* and of the best quality—if it had been otherwise, it might not so readily have obtained the favour which it now enjoys , a circumstance of trifling consequence to appearance, but very important in its results , for to this cause might, in a great measure, be attributed the enormous crops that have been raised the past year, amounting to forty, fifty, and even sixty tons per acre, with roots of twenty-seven pounds each in weight †

Frank Well now, would it not be very easy for you to sketch a mode of farming upon paper, and make a map of a convenient sized farm, with arrangements for suitable buildings, and every thing as it should be? to be sure it would only be *farming upon paper*, which is, however, as many of our poor neighbours would now confess, the easiest kind of farming , but still, a life of practical observation must afford the means of rendering even that interesting to many

Father Well then, suppose we see what can be done in the way of *farming upon paper* You see we shall enjoy great advantages, first, we shall be

* The difference in the quantity of saccharine matter contained in the varieties of the beet, is often as twelve to two

† W Andenreed raised 62½ tons sugar-beet per acre, in Schuylkill County, Pennsylvania.—*American Farmer's Instructor*

able to obtain, without money, just as much land, and of the quality we wish, and in the pleasantest situation imaginable, with facilities for fencing and cultivating it to our hearts' content , no impediment to our progress, and within reach of every desirable object—churches, schools, and markets, as the advertisements say Still I believe, although only upon paper, that such a plan might be made interesting even to the practical agriculturist, and from which he might possibly be able to reap a new idea—which would be doing much Now, in the outset, I must tell you, I mean to farm according to the " new school," the first rule being, to possess no more land than you can properly manage , and as I know at this time a farm of twenty-five acres, which yields more produce, greater in quantity and infinitely better in quality than the adjoining farm of one hundred and fifty acres of exactly the same natural quality of soil, I shall confine myself to a square of land of one hundred acres, pleasantly located, of course, and of good quality, cleared (for I fear we should not be good at chopping), but not fenced

Frank Well, father, I long to be at it

Father You see already the advantage of farming upon paper, for by taking a square of land with nothing to obstruct our plans, we shall be able to throw all our enclosures into the most convenient form and size without the least difficulty , namely, in the first instance into four fields of sixteen acres each, four of eight acres each, and one of four acres, exactly in the centre of the farm, in which are to be placed the buildings of every description, farm-yards, garden orchard, &c according to the following plan.

Fig 1

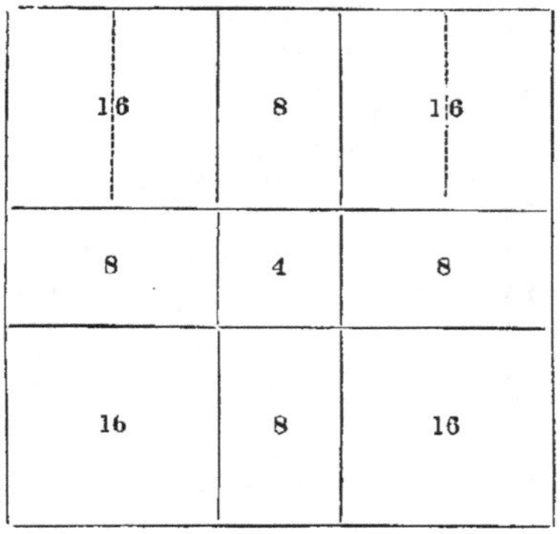

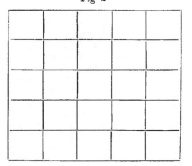

Fig 2

Now a square of land measuring seven hundred yards each way, contains one hundred acres, and about an acre and a quarter as space for fences The outer fence should be made first, after which, the four inner fences, by which simple operation the whole land will at once be divided, according to the plan Fig 1 Cultivate at first, the four fields of eight acres each only, the course of crops being roots, oats, clover, wheat. The four fields of sixteen acres each might, in the mean time, remain in grass, being top-dressed with marl, lime, or compost, and fed with cattle or sheep, these to be regularly changed from pasture to pasture, upon those fields not devoted to the hay-crops, one or two of them being, however, devoted to this purpose And when, at a future time, it should be desirable to subdivide these fields to bring them into cultivation, two walls or fences, carried in the direction of the dotted line, will do the business effectually and very conveniently, bringing four more fields, or double the quantity of land, into cultivation another like division of the two remaining fields of sixteen acres each, throws the whole farm into fields of eight acres, of the most convenient form for til-lage, with every fence straight, and all surrounding the homestead

These subdivisions can, however, be continued, until all the fields are square, and contain just four acres each, according to the plan Fig 2.

Frank Well, this would be delightful! Why, one hundred acres of land thus laid out, would be a large farm, twenty-four fields of four acres each, with a square of four acres in the centre for gardens,

17*

orchards, yards, buildings, and sheds—who need
desire more?

Father. I admit that as much produce could be
obtained from these one hundred acres, highly cultivated and heavily manured, and devoted to the
growth of useful crops—not weeds—as from farms
of five times the size, whose owners conceive that
"land won't pay for good management," and where
one half of it is devoted to the production of weeds
and what is called *timber*, which is often mere rubbish So far our first rule of the "new school,"
namely, to possess no more land than you can properly cultivate

The second rule is, never to go out of the reach of
society and good markets—two things of incalculable weight and importance I have many friends
who have gone and buried themselves, their families,
and their talents, not in a napkin, but in a desert,
because they were determined to get *cheap land*,
without considering that in these places produce is
cheap likewise Poor Joe B——, who went some
time since to Michigan Territory to farm, because
there every thing is so cheap—beef three and a half
cents per pound, butter eight cents per pound, wheat
half a dollar a bushel, mutton dog cheap, and wood
for cutting! before this Joe has found his wits, *if he
has not lost them* Always remember,

> The worth of a thing
> Is as much as 'twill bring,

and no more, and if land sells for a dollar an acre,
'tis a clear proof that it is worth no more, else it would

bring it I calculate that land very near a good
market is worth, to an intelligent and industrious
man, many times the mere rent, on the simple account, that the farmer need be but little from home
I declare I have known the time when I would not
leave home a day for a quarter's rent, and then,
only calculate the value of the time spent in travelling
by night and *by day* a distance of perhaps seventeen
or twenty miles to market, to say nothing of the
extreme irksomeness, pain and suffering attendant
upon such a *pilgrimage*, exposed to the vicissitudes
of the seasons—heat and cold, and rain and wind!
Oh, it is sickening to think what a great portion of
such a man's life is thus disposed of!

Frank Well then, as we are, you know, farming
upon paper, we can fix our farm just where we
choose, it will be in no one's way now how near a
good market would you like it to be?

Father Say six miles—an easy hour from market
And now, as we find we can do pretty much as we
like, what do you say to the following mode of farming one hundred acres of land, so as to make the
most of it, and at the same time not to make a toil
of what ought to be a pleasure We will suppose
that we have erected upon our middle compartment,
1 A comfortable dwelling-house, with dairy, &c
attached, garden, orchard, &c 2 A good barn
3 Warm stables 4 Cow sheds 5 Sheds for
young stock 6 Fatting sheds for sheep 7 Fatting
stalls for oxen 8 Hogsties 9 Granary and tool-
house 10 Cart and implement shed, and plenty of
yard room

Now, as I should be desirous of going gently forward, and as, after all this, our *means might be slender*, you know, I would propose to cultivate at first the four fields of eight acres only, top-dressing with lime-compost the four fields of sixteen acres at our leisure, and feeding and mowing them alternately And if by *tip top* management we could raise on the first of these eight acre fields three hundred and twenty tons of Silesian beets, forty tons per acre,* on the second field a crop of oats about four feet in height, which, if threshed, would yield sixty bushels per acre, in all four hundred and twenty bushels, on the third, thirty tons of clover-hay, at two cuttings, and on the fourth, eight loads of thrashed wheat, with plenty of straw for the bedding of horses, and cattle of all kinds—would you not think we had done well?

Frank Well? Ah, but there, 'tis only on paper, you know!

Father True, but " nothing is impossible to a will-

---

* The sugar-beet should be sown on land well pulverized by deep ploughing in the autumn and thorough spring working Ridge up the land into one-bout ridges at the distance approved for the rows, and in the trenches place the dung in as large a quantity as can be afforded, then split the ridges with the plough, throwing the earth right and left on the dung, and on the ridges so formed, drill the seed and roll it—real hot-bed culture.

When the plants are sufficiently grown to admit of thinning, the plan pursued by the late Mr Geo Walker, of Holmesburg, is perhaps the best that can be adopted. A man with a broad hoe goes over the rows, when children follow, and selecting the strongest plants, take each in the left hand, by way of security, and with the right, pull away the remainder setting the single plant upright by a gentle pressure about it—thus completing the work as they go The expense is not great, when spread over a crop of forty five tons per acre, but the profit is. The after hoeing must, of course, be well attended to, but no moulding up is necessary

---

ing mind," *you know;* such crops have absolutely been obtained, and " what man *has* done, man *may* do ," and as our exertions would be so concentrated, and we should be called so seldom from home, I should not despair of *doing likewise*, and I would not willingly go for less than the *whole hog* Now, as the stock would graze during the summer the four fields of sixteen acres each, except that part which might be set apart for mowing hay, we should be able to reserve the whole of the crops of the four cultivated fields for winter use—an enormous mass of food, and yet grown upon a very small quantity of land So you see, the only crop we should have to take to the market would be the thrashed wheat—the most saleable of all the crops, requiring only to be delivered at the mill

Frank Well, this would be simplifying the system, truly

Father Yes, but I should not doubt of perfect success in this " new system of farming," for the feeding of such a quantity of winter food, would produce manure sufficient to make the land *as rich as a cucumber bed*, as the saying is, for I should propose to expend it all on the beet and clover crops, sixteen acres only Thus the oats would have none, for they would not require any, nor the wheat, which would be injured by it, and thus our system would be perfect, according to the rules of modern husbandry namely, " two grain crops not to follow in succession, and the manure to be applied solely for the production of food for the cattle,"—the two golden rules of the " new school " The produce of such a farm, in the shape of beef mutton, veal, lamb, and butter, would be contained in small compass, and be market-ed with little expense and labour, time or trouble, while the expenses of cultivation would be compara-tively very small, as the only thrashing would be the wheat crop, the only part of the crops to be carried to market.   The necessary quantity of ploughing would be singularly small, it being for the beets three or four, oats once, and that before Christmas, none for the clover, and once only for the wheat forty-eight acres only during the year   The only hoeing would be on the beet crop, which must not have a weed growing on it, requiring the labour of the horse as well as the hand-hoe, while the harvest-ing would be light and easily accomplished

Frank Well, the hours of attendance in this "new school" would be but few

Father True, but they would be fully occupied still, although, I grant you, pleasantly   And as soon as the four fields of eight acres each have been made as rich as possible by culture and manure, instead of becoming exhausted, then will be the time to take a portion, say one field of sixteen acres, of the pasture land into cultivation, which, having been dressed with lime-compost and fed, will come under the plough in so fresh and inexhausted a state, as to produce enor-mous crops, the first being oats

By a plan such as the above, I calculate that a man would be able to obtain the means of living even from one hundred acres of land, and I guess he ought to be happy, for his labours would be very much lightened by the simplicity of the course pur-sued

Much has been said on the best mode of fencing, and the materials most proper for the purpose when stone can be obtained, there is nothing to be at all compared with stone walls, their expense in erection is great, but their security, strength, durability, and the shelter which they afford in stormy weather, are above all price " they are major from the first," as some one says, and when they require repair, the means are at hand, just where they have fallen, at the foot of the wall, ready to be replaced in an instant Posts and rails—the timber for which ought to be cut in the summer and dried by fire, which may be made for the purpose in the saw-pit, over which the posts, &c may be piled, and by which means their durability for a great length of time is secured, as by it they are rendered *worm-proof*—come next in value, as they require no tedious time to await their coming to maturity But living fences when well grown and kept clean and carefully trimmed, are more beautiful, they are excellent to be sure, but it would be a laborious undertaking to fence a farm with living hedges, and I fear I should not be willing to commence so long and tedious a labour, small portions, however, around the house and garden might be planted, and they will, when well grown, add beauty to the scenery

A very neat paling might be put up around the house with the staves of sugar hogsheads, which, in many places, might be obtained in any quantity, and at a low price, before putting up, they should be washed with hot lime-water, which will add much to their durability, and while hot, they might be easily straightened, and by selecting them according to their width, sharpening them at one end, and resting their other ends on a foot wide board nailed on its edge from post to post, this would give the fence a respectable appearance, and do away the suspicion that it is nothing more than a *sugar hogshead fence*

An excellent and very cheap paint with which to cover them, as well as other wood-work exposed to the weather, is made by taking three parts slaked lime while dry, one of clean fine sand, and two of clean wood-ashes, sift the whole together and add as much linseed oil as will be necessary to reduce the composition, when well mixed, to such consistence that it may be applied with a brush The wood requires only two coats, the first may be thin, but the second, which should not be put on until the first is dry, should be as thick as the brush can lay it on This coating, when well prepared, is impenetrable to water, and resists the influence of the weather and the action of the sun, which hardens and renders it more durable

The strongest plaster for covering walls which are peculiarly exposed to the weather, and which will render them impenetrable, is called " The mastic of the Greeks," and is made with the following articles clean, dry, sharp sand, dry white-lead and litharge mixed well and very intimately with linseed oil, so as to fit it to work easily with the trowel, it must be particularly well worked when laid on, and finished by hard rubbing with the tool Nothing gives so fine and smooth a surface, and when quite dry, it resists even a nail when driven with the hammer The

proper proportions of the ingredients will easily be found, when the fineness or coarseness of the work desired, has been decided upon

If milk be added to lime white-wash for inside work, it will be found to adhere to the walls, and will not rub off, it will also be much smoother and more easily laid on, as the alkali of the lime when coming in contact with the oleaginous quality of the milk, forms a kind of soap, which works somewhat like white lead paint

----

DIALOGUE XVII

DAIRYING

Frank Father, if you were to describe in the Farmers' Cabinet, the way in which you manage your dairy, I think it likely that some persons would consider about it, and take the trouble to try your plan, and see if it would prove more advantageous than their own

Father In that I think you are mistaken In the business of the dairy, there is, I believe, more confidence felt and expressed than in any other branch of husbandry every one thinks his own mode of operation the best, and often, without the means of knowing how others pursue that branch of their calling, have long determined upon a plan for themselves, which they would feel it very unpleasant or even difficult to relinquish And you must have observed with what determination our neighbours stick to their own methods, although they see that we always sell out our butter at the market before them, and at an uniformly higher price

Frank I have observed that, and although I last week heard John Ross's mother make the same remark, and wonder how it should be, I am sure she knows why it is, but cannot determine to quit the old method which she has pursued through life I am led to think about this just now, from the observation which I heard one of our customers make the last market-day, he was recommending our butter to a friend, and assured him he had kept some of it six weeks, and at the end of that time it was perfectly sweet and good, when his friend said, " Aye, I have kept it longer than that, and still it was as good as ever " So I wish you would describe your method, which might be made applicable to our snug little farm of one hundred acres, you know; there are some, perhaps, who would put it into practice, if it were only for the curiosity of the thing

Father Well, if from no better motive, I should be quite content if they would do so, only out of curiosity, for *I too* think my own way the best

But I consider that the business of the dairy commences with the stables in which the cows are kept, these are often placed in some damp and shady situation for the sake of being near to water, and by this the health of the cows is often very seriously affected —this is highly improper The situation of the stables should be dry and airy, and facing a little towards the east, so that the sun might shine full into the door

at eleven o'clock, sufficient shelter can be obtained by good high fencing about the yard, and the best water is that which is supplied from a pump in the stable, so that the cows might drink warm water— not iced water—in the winter, and cool water in the summer, and always get it sweet and clean, an important item in dairying The approach for feeding should always be at the heads of the cows, and they should stand on a platform a little sloping, about three or four inches in height, with a wide gutter passing behind them, well paved, along which the dung might easily be swept, and be conveyed away to the pit outside the building Each cow should be furnished with a rack and manger, and a short partition at the head of each, forms the best security The sliding ring on an upright pole, with a leather collar, or strap, and buckle attached, is preferable to every other mode of tying

Frank Well, this is just the plan of our cow-stables, and we know how convenient they are, and how clean our cows are kept during winter, compared with those of our neighbours

Father True, this is the first step in the business, the next is, never to keep a cow in the dairy that is decidedly unprofitable Few persons are aware of the immense difference which there is between cows in the products of the dairy, even when fed and managed in every respect in the same way, a very few unprofitable cows will soon reduce the whole concern to poverty And I am sometimes amused to read the statements in books, on the profits of a dairy, without the knowledge or experience on the part of the writers, that there is often about one hundred per cent difference in the value of cows in the same dairy Now there is our neighbour Ross, in general a man of excellent judgment, but upon this subject as thoughtless as a child, for he does not, I am sure, obtain from his large dairy half the quantity of butter that we do from ours, while the quality, and the price which we obtain, is still greatly in our favour On examination, one half the number of his cows would be found worse than useless, for they do not pay for their keep These are those that he has reared from old favourite cows* of no value in the dairy, but, as *members of the family*, have been looked up to with a sort of veneration for many years, exhibiting all the marks of an unprofitable breed for milk, hardy, perhaps, with a tendency to fatten, and to this purpose they ought to be consigned without mercy Now compare these animals with our Judy, Kate, and Nell, from which, as you know, we have for many weeks past, made twelve pounds of butter each, and who exhibit in their forms every quality of great milkers, namely, the thin and soft skin and hair, light limbs, small head, and thin neck, with udder large and full, but after milking, more like white leather bags to the sight and touch, and above all, narrow loins and rump, for, according to our friend the Dishley sheep-breeder, this must be a mark of the greatest importance, if, as he says, "when an animal is narrow across the back, the juices flow over it and settle in the belly, while on a

* Old proverb, 'The calf of a young cow, the pig of an old sow," i e for the purpose of rearing stock

wide and full loin they remain, and go to produce flesh and fat " These are the cows for a dairy, and will pay for *keeping*, but not, even they, for *starving*

Frank But the pure Durhams, of which we hear so much, and which cost so much too, are very different in their forms, and yet, according to account their yield of milk and butter is enormous

Father True, they might be called artificial cows, and by treating them artificially, they have been made to perform wonders, but I would not fear comparison with those of ours above mentioned, under the same circumstances, quantity of butter for food consumed And there would be a very peculiar difference observable in the quality of the milk and butter, of these enormously large and fat beasts when compared with that from ours—extremely rich, of course, but with a peculiarity of flavour, and partaking of a meaty consistence very discernible to a delicate taste—no disparagement, however, is meant, they are noble animals, but in my estimation, better suited for the cheese than the butter dairy, and only pay when their keep is high and strong

Frank Then, I begin to see that a great difference in the advantage and profit of a dairy, must arise from the kind of cows which are kept, independent of the cost and kind of food which they consume, and I can now understand, why it is that our neighbours have remarked the peculiar fragrance of our butter, observable on opening the churn, just as the butter is "come"—they have attributed it to the fine

18*

pasture of our cows, which, as they remark, being free from weeds, the butter must of course be more free from bad taste and smell

Father This is, no doubt the fact, but with a different breed of cows, even this grand and important item would not make all the difference, for it is but natural, that the milk of an animal must partake, in a very especial manner, of the juices and peculiar constitution of that animal, and it stands to reason that the produce of a large, fat, *beefy* cow must be more coarse and strong-flavoured, than that of such as Judy, Kate, and Nell, whose very breath is like the newly-mown hay

Frank I have often been astonished, to see the cows that are generally kept by our neighbours, when driven into the yards to be milked, and to observe so little difference in the size of their udders after the operation, when they are again turned to pasture, I believe that some of them do not produce two pounds of butter a week

Father I dare say they do not, but this is only a part of the evil, for it is almost uniformly the case, that the milk of cows which yield so little, is inferior in quality, and oftentimes extremely nauseous in flavour, being produced from a different part of the animal, than that which is drawn from great milkers, and is often contaminated with the impurities of that system, drawn away at the time of milking Now there are our neighbour Ticey's cows, they are all large and fat, but when I compare his dairy account with mine, I find they do not yield near the quantity of butter that ours do, and are dry for three months

in the year, while you know that our cows would never go dry of themselves.

Frank. Yes, I know that, for you remember that Kate calved within two days of our ceasing to milk her, and all the while her milk was perfectly sweet

Father True, and when I have endeavoured to persuade Ticey to exchange his large cows for those of a smaller breed, he has said "But only calculate their value for fatting, after I have done with them in the dairy!" "Yes," said I, "three or four years hence, but after I have obtained eight, ten or twelve pounds of butter per week from a cow for seven or eight years, I can credit her a little on that score, while you do nothing with yours for about that time" No man in his *right* senses will keep a bad milker to rob him of his profits, better sell for almost *nothing*, and buy for almost *any thing*, and keep an account of the profit and loss of the transaction

Frank Well, now for the butter and milk account I long to come to that

Father And so it seems, but you are forestalling the business, you seem to have forgotten, that the cows have not yet been fed and properly attended; two little items in a dairy account, that, insignificant as you might consider them, are, I assure you, of great weight in our future calculations

And now, I confess I should be at a loss to know how to provide through the winter, for a dairy of cows, on so small a farm as thirty-two acres arable, were it not for the introduction of the sugar-beet into cultivation, that crop has, however, enabled us, as I have said, to do *what* we wish and *all* that we wish, for by proper management, a store of roots might be raised for the full supply of at least two-thirds of the year—from September to May—or even longer, if it should be found necessary. Much has been *said and sung* about the best method of preserving them for winter use, nothing is more easy; for if they are buried so deep as to be out of the influence of the atmosphere, they might be kept perfectly sound and good for any length of time, and without vegetating. For the purpose of sugar-making, it is quite necessary that fermentation, whether arising from heat or vegetation, should be guarded against, but for the feeding of cattle, this is not of so much importance; this, however, as well as injury from frost, might be totally prevented by burying deep. To this end, therefore, I would propose to dig a cellar under the cow-stables, to receive those roots that are designed to be fed to the cattle during the autumn and early part of the winter, while another cellar, immediately adjoining—and to which access might be had by means of a door from thence—deep, and arched with brick, and covered thick with earth, and of sufficient capacity to contain the remainder of the stock of roots, should be formed outside the stables, with a round hole in the crown of the arch, through which the roots might be let carefully down, as they are brought by the carts. This hole should be closed and well covered with earth, as soon as the cellar is filled, and over it, a low and slight shed might be built, in which to fodder young stock and sheep. After the roots in the first cellar—that under

the cow-stable—are expended, a quantity, sufficient for a few days, might be taken from the inner cellar, and be deposited there for present use, so that the door need not be opened oftener than about once a week, care being taken to block it well with earth, after being properly closed. With such a stock of roots and hay, and oats cut in the straw, no one need dread a winter of any length or severity. It will not be necessary to cut the roots, even for young cattle or sheep, but an attachment might be made to the threshing machine, if there be one, for cutting up the oats in the straw, and the same gearing might be used in churning the butter, or a small horse-wheel might be erected for these purposes, which would be found a most valuable appendage to the establishment, saving much time, labour, and expense.

And now for the milk and butter, or rather, first the milk-house, which, it is *not* indispensable, should be erected over a spring, for with my mode of management, this is not, as you know, necessary; but it should be situated on the shady side of the dwelling, and be well covered with trees, with the means of obtaining a thorough current of air when necessary. And during the heat of summer, a current of cold air might be obtained by means of a bricked arch or tunnel, running for some distance under the ground, and communicating with the external air in some shaded situation, passing under the wall of the milk-house, and rising, by a grated aperture, in the centre of the floor. No arrangement might be made for the introduction of water, for—and here is the peculiarity of our method—no water is ever permitted to come in contact with the milk, or cream, or butter, at any stage of the process of butter-making The utensils, and every part of the milk-house, the shelves, and even the floor, are to be washed clean with hot water, and to be immediately rubbed dry, not being left to evaporate the moisture in the dairy, every part being kept as dry as possible at all seasons of the year

The milk-pans, two only in number, made of zinc after a particular pattern, and managed in a peculiar way, deserve a particular description

Double milk-pans, for large or small dairies

These pans, made of zinc, possess many and great advantages over those in general use, and are recommended, as far superior to any ever before adopted, for the purpose of raising the cream, and facilitating the labours of the dairy

1 They are peculiarly strong in their construction, not liable to get out of order, are most convenient in their form, and take but little room in the milk-house

2 They communicate no unpleasant flavour to the milk, are most easily kept clean by means of hot water, a brush, and soap, requiring not a tenth part of the labour necessary to keep others sweet, and are suitable for all seasons and situations

3 They are made of different sizes, to suit large or small dairies, the largest being sufficiently capacious to contain the milk of many cows, indeed— unless the dairy be very large—the milk of all, it having been found advantageous, both to the quantity

and quality of the butter, to mix together milk of different cows, at the time of setting it to cream

4. At the time of skimming, the labour of collecting the cream from those pans, is not a twentieth part of that necessary where pans of any other construction are used, while all the cream and none of the milk is obtained, with the greatest precision, and without trouble

5 The business of churning is much facilitated, the butter "coming" very quickly, and this takes place in a regular way, uninfluenced, in a great measure, by seasons or circumstances, the cream having been submitted to the same process and degree of heat, is uniform in its aptitude to "butter"

6 The butter is uniform in quality, and of a marrowy consistence, never so hard and flinty in winter, and in summer, requiring only the usual care, to preserve it firm and cool, while it is remarkable in the property of keeping sweet for any reasonable length of time, and being always of a superior colour to that made from the same cream in the usual way A calculation has been made, that a pound of butter can be obtained per week from each cow, more by this process than by any other

Description of the pans, and mode of using them

Each pan is placed on a strong wooden frame, of the most convenient height It is dish-shaped, either square or oblong The largest size might be about five feet six inches long, by thirty inches wide, smaller pans and of different sizes can be made to order They are double, the pan for containing the milk, being firmly joined to another of the same shape, but somewhat larger, which forms a casing around it, the space between them, being from one to two inches deep, is for the purpose of containing hot water, thus forming a hot bath around the milk. In the centre of the upper, or milk-pan, which dips regularly from all parts towards the middle, is a fine strainer, formed by punching very small holes through the zinc, in a circle about two inches diameter, and to this is soldered a short pipe, which reaches through the bottom of the casing pan, of which, however, it is independent this pipe is furnished with a brass tap, its purpose being to let off the milk contained in the upper pan, at the end of the process The casing or *bottom* pan, is furnished with two pipes, one of these perforates a corner of the upper or milk-pan, and through it, boiling water is poured, by means of a funnel—with the pipe of it a little flattened, to permit the air to escape while pouring in the water—at the proper time, so as completely to fill the space between the pans, thus, as has been said, forming a hot bath around the milk By the other pipe, at the bottom, furnished also with a tap, the water is let off at the proper season Thus the pans, although firmly joined together, are independent of each other, the union, however, strengthening each, in a remarkable manner

At the time of milking, the taps are closed, and the upper pan is filled with milk as it is brought from the cows, after standing twelve hours, the tap of this pan is partially unclosed, and a small portion of the milk is drawn off, this, on examination, will be found

to contain the impurities of the milk which have subsided, the peculiar formation of the pan having induced the sediment to form exactly on the strainer, and this economy is of much consequence to the quality of the butter The *casing*, or bottom pan, is then filled with boiling water,* by means of the pipe, which perforates the upper or milk pan, which pipe is then to be closed, and the water is permitted to stand twelve hours, when it is drawn off, by placing a vessel to receive it and opening the tap below, first unclosing the upper pipe, to give it vent After this, the *milk* is drawn off, every particle of the cream having risen to the surface, and the milk will be found to drain away, leaving the cream in the pan, from whence it can be removed with the greatest ease and facility very little practice in this part of the process will make perfect.

As soon, however, as the cream is removed, the pan must be well washed with hot water, a brush, and soap, which will neutralize any acidity which there might be, and a careful rinsing and dry rubbing after, fits it for an immediate re-filling, without removal or labour The cream might now be transferred to the churn, where it will soon become butter of the finest quality, or it might be "brought," by merely stirring with the hand in a pan, after the De-

* The heat of the water which is first poured into the pan, will be considerably reduced by coming into contact with the cold pans, this therefore should be let off after standing awhile and be replaced by other, boiling hot. I have found the first water to raise the heat of the milk to 108 degrees

vonshire method ; either way, which is thought most convenient The churn is never used on many of the dairy farms in Devonshire

REMARKS

This is a new, interesting, and convenient process of butter making, the advantages of which are scarcely to be appreciated, but which cannot be fully carried out without the use of double milk-pans Every housekeeper is aware of the advantage of scalding or cooking the milk, intended to be kept until the following day, and by the means above described, this process is conducted in the simplest manner, without labour or inconvenience, and with the greatest precision , the mode being an improvement on that which is practised in Devonshire, which is, at the end of twelve hours, to take every pan of milk to a hot plate, where it must remain " a given time," to be ascertained by unwearied watchfulness, and, on the signal being observed, it must instantly be removed, and taken back to its former place, after which, however, it is often found to have acquired a disagreeable burnt flavour from over-cooking, sufficient to spoil the finest butter , while the milk that has been submitted to the heat of a hot water bath, will be found to have deposited every particle of its cream on the surface, without having acquired any bad or unpleasant flavour The milk of some cows is known, never properly to separate its cream, but by this process, first of mixing all the milk of the dairy, and then submitting it to the hot water bath, every particle of cream is raised, and to this circum-

stance is to be attributed, in a measure, the extra quantity of butter which is always obtained by this management   The cream too, remains much longer sweet, and acquires an aptitude to " butter," which is truly surprising, rendering unnecessary that incessant beating into foam for twenty-four hours—as every dairyman has wofully experienced—by which the butter is rendered hot and rancid, even before it is taken from the churn.

But perhaps one of the greatest and most perceptible advantages of these pans is, the owner of the dairy is no longer at the mercy of careless and unprincipled servants, who, in the hurry of skimming, are often known to sacrifice a great portion of cream to the hog-tub—a loss which soon amounts to a great consideration—here, these servants have only to set the milk-pans running, and they will skim themselves, requiring only a little care to stop them when the milk has passed away , while a very serious injury is prevented which arises from the opposite vice— that of over-skimming, by which the butter is often deteriorated by the stale milk, which is thus taken and mixed with the cream , for if the strainer be of the proper size and fineness, the milk will all pass, and the cream will all remain

To a nice observer, however, the means of drawing off the impurities of the milk at the bottom of the pan before adding the boiling water, will not be lightly considered ; a close examination of this portion of the milk will convince any one, by smell as well as by taste, that nothing is so disgusting as ani-

mal putricity The skim-milk, from this process, is
peculiarly sweet, nearly equal to new milk to the taste,
and very superior for the making of cheese

Frank Well now, a thought has just struck me—
I believe that milk is the only animal substance which
is taken in a raw state into the stomach No, oysters
are eaten raw, but I believe nothing *animal* besides
And the butter which is made from raw cream—that
is raw likewise, for in no part of the process of
making, does it undergo the operation of cooking,
and yet *new milk* is recommended to infants and
delicate females, and to persons in the last stage of
sickness, without considering the very great probability there is, that in its raw state it might be very
injurious to such delicate and weakly constitutions, to
say nothing of the great probability that that which is
produced by rank, large, *beefy* cattle, of coarse, un-
healthy, and humoury constitutions, might be used
for this purpose—the thought is nauseous and disgusting Now cooking would be, in this case, of great
importance

Father A new idea, and a very important one,
and a strong recommendation of our new process of
butter-making

The plump churn, which we use for twenty-five or
thirty pounds of butter, is of the Welsh pattern, with
swelling, not straight sides, this gives the cream more
space, and the agitation is greater and more easily
communicated, and when the cream thickens, still
there is room for the plunger to work, consequently
the labour is much lessened

In putting the cream into the churn, it is very customary to wash the cream-pans with water, and add
it to the cream in the churn, this should be avoided,
as you would avoid poison—not a drop of water must
come in contact with the cream or butter, from first
to last And when the butter is "come," it is customary to pour off a part of the butter-milk, add water,
and churn again, to beat the butter together, and in
part, to wash it—this is worse still, for the water
carries away with it the fragrance of the butter, and
gives it a tendency to early rancidity If the butter
requires to be beaten together in the churn, no water
should be added on any account, after letting off the
butter-milk. On taking the butter out of the churn,
it should be beaten, in lumps about two pounds each,
on a thick piece of very smooth, hard board, with the
edges rounded off, held in the left hand by a knob on
the under side, with a flat and thick piece of wood,
formed somewhat like the sole of a shoe, very hard
and smooth, and furnished with a handle, and on a
single trial, every one will be convinced that every
particle of the milk can be driven out, without washing with water After this, it is to be spread on a
table or smooth board, and salted, then rolled together, and divided into lumps about a pound each,
and beaten again, and it is then fit for the print.
The following cut represents a neat, convenient, and
cleanly little contrivance for this purpose, which
ought to be introduced to general notice, as it saves
the necessity of *handling* the butter while print-
ing it

Description

" The butter-stamp consists of a small round box, fastened to a square piece of deal, through the bottom of which is a hole for the introduction of the handle of a second box, which fits within the first The second box is similar to the first, except that it is detached from the bottom, and consists of three pieces of wood, hollowed out, and made to shut close to each other, like the leaves of a flower-cup When the handle with the bottom attached, is drawn down, the three pieces or leaves fall into a groove running around the second box The butter is weighed and placed in the box, the handle being down, the stamp or print is then placed on the top of the butter, and forced down hard, giving it the proper shape and print, after which it is turned out complete, by forcing the bottom up, by means of the handle, seen in the figure, which causes the second box to fall apart, as it were, and thus the butter is released

" Fig A represents the mould with the butter in it, the stamp on, and all ready for forcing out B, one

of the sides or leaves of the three-sided inner box C, the bottom, with handle "

And now, if those who think that the butter-milk cannot be extracted without washing with water, will try the above mode of management and working, and put a portion of the butter away for a month or two, and examine it at the end of that time, they will be quite convinced—of a good many things

Frank Is not the Island of Jersey famous for good butter ? Our friend, W P , told us, you may remember, that while he resided in Rio Janeiro they ate Jersey butter as fresh as though it had been made but the day before Now, how could it be conveyed to such a distance, and into such a hot climate, without becoming rancid and oily ?

Father I was told of a captain of a vessel, who engaged to take butter to Rio Janeiro from Jersey, and that it might be as much as possible out of the influence of the heat of the climate, especially while crossing the line, he placed the barrels containing it at the bottom of the hold of the ship On arriving at his port and looking for his butter, he found that not a *drop* of it remained in the barrels—it had all escaped, and was found amongst the ballast, from whence it was removed by means of shovels! The way they now transport it is, to press it, with very little salt, into tight barrels, which are then well headed up, and these are placed in larger barrels, with a covering of salt, well rammed in, they are then carefully headed up, and it is found that no heat will penetrate through a covering of salt, even during the longest voyage

The quality of the Jersey (Island) butter, arises rather from the delicacy of the breed of cows, than from the food which they eat, for on some of their very small farms, the supply is so short, that at certain seasons they are compelled to put up with very coarse fare. The high-bred Durhams show their origin and aptitude for milk and butter which they inherit, from the *Alderneys*, as they are called, although the handsomest and most valuable animals of this breed come from Jersey—an island within sight of those of Guernsey and Alderney, but the breed of its cattle is very different from that of either of them

———

DIALOGUE XVIII

BLIGHT

Frank Father, as I passed Farmer Ticey's orchard this morning, I saw him busily employed making a fire of wet straw on the windward side of his orchard, that the smoke might prevent the ill effects of the fog on his apple-trees, while Farmer Vince stood by, laughing at him for his pains. I have often thought to ask you to tell me the cause of blight

Father This is a subject of great importance, and it has engaged the attention of great men for ages, the question is still, however, as far as ever from being decided, for the advocates of the different

systems are so nicely balanced that it is difficult to know who have the preponderance I confess, however, that to me it appears easy to be understood by persons of practical observation, we will, therefore, examine it, and perhaps we may discover how it is that persons differ so widely on so plain a subject.

Frank I have always heard that blight is brought by the cold winds and damp air, but it is strange that these little insects should delight in such weather, and go abroad at a time when all other creatures prefer staying at home! so that, according to this theory, the cold weather in summer gives life to insects, while the cold weather in winter destroys them.

Father I too, believe that the cold weather in spring and summer is the *cause* of blight, but these little insects are the *consequences*, or the *effects* of the cold—so that the *effect* has been taken for the *cause*—that's all You have heard of the perspiration of plants—now, when a cold blast arises in the spring or summer, it is often attended with mist or damp air, which is vapour condensed and rendered visible by the cold, perspiration is checked by this cold air, and then the sap becomes stagnant, other sap arising however from the body of the plant or tree, these corrupt juices are forced out through the pores of the leaves in the form of honey-dew, and growing putrid, they soon become loaded with living animalculæ, for, as is said by numerous writers, " *all putrid substances engender life*" These little creatures then, feed upon the corrupt juices of the plant, and in seeking for them, puncture the leaves in every direction, and at length attack them wholesale, and leave nothing but the rib-work behind them, and then they die for want of food   Often, however, their ravages are arrested by a warm shower, which, restoring the circulation of the sap, brings on returning perspiration, and then, the juices becoming purified, are again taken up into circulation, and being no longer fit for the support of the life of these creatures who feed only on putricity, they die another kind of death

Now, we know how apt we are to take cold by exposure to a current of cold or damp air during a state of perspiration, and also, how sensible we are of its effects on the constitution—how soon blotches appear on the skin, and particularly the breaking out on the lips—this might be aptly compared to the exuding of the corrupt juices through the pores of the leaves of plants, and as a warm shower is sure to have the effect of restoring the circulation of the sap, and destroying the insects on those plants, so a warm bath has been found of the greatest effect in restoring lost circulation in the human body

But if these insects are brought ready made in the cold air, what a great variety of them there must be, floating about at the same time! for it is observable that almost every tree and plant has its peculiar species of insect or blight, you know

Frank Now I think I understand that perfectly, and whenever I again see plants affected by the blight, I shall say they have *taken cold !*

Father Yes, and now I suppose you can understand how it is that the young and tender plants are more liable to suffer from colds, than their older and more robust brethren—the wheat that is sown in the

spring, than that which is sown in the autumn   But it will be exceedingly interesting to witness the effects of one of these cold, damp, and blighting winds in the spring or summer on vegetation, in almost an instant you will perceive a change of colour on the leaves, which will at length become blue, and soon after, small insects will appear in the shape of little round balls on the surface, as though they were eggs in clusters, these very soon come to life, but how they have been engendered, is at present a mystery—we only know the fact, that it is so

I remember once meeting with a venerable man, a minister, with whom I fell into conversation on this subject, he said, " In the year 18— a general blight took place all over England, it was preceded by a cold and moist wind from the northeast, which continued to blow for some days in the month of April, and I knew how it would be—in a few days, almost every leaf upon the plants and trees was covered with insects of every form and colour, like the elephant, the rhinoceros, even down to the mouse, and of every tint of the rainbow   people began to be exceedingly terrified, and expected nothing less than the plague, and it was then remembered, that the plague of London was ushered in by such a general blight—it was awfully alarming—I remember an excellent and pious lady, one of my congregation, calling upon me, to request that I would offer up a prayer on the following Sabbath, that the Almighty would be pleased to avert from us so dreadful a scourge, which I most gladly and devoutly promised to do, and prepared accordingly   before the day appointed, the Almighty had taken the thing in hand himself, and did the business so effectually, that by the next Sabbath, not an insect was to be seen, they had all vanished—the Lord only knew where' It was, I think, on a Monday that the lady called on me, and on that very night there fell so awful and tremendous a thunderstorm, and a second deluge of rain, which prevented the necessity of *prayer*, so we changed the subject, and had a most glorious day of *praise and thanksgiving* on the day of our appointed humiliation —but the interposition was so great and signal, that the effects were visible on the parishioners, in their general conduct I mean, for years, I may say until the present time" Now all these *effects* were *caused* by obstructed circulation, which produced stagnation of the juices, and then followed corruption, which engendered life Remember, the immediate cause of blight is a sudden change of the atmosphere from heat to piercing cold, which instantaneously closes the pores, and obstructs the circulation of the sap Now is not this clear enough?

Frank I should think so, for I have often witnessed just such *effects* from just such *causes* I know, now that you have pointed them out to me

Father An excellent writer observes, "the sagacious Tull, for want of having thoroughly considered the subject, has fallen in with this popular notion, and has mistaken the *effect* for the *cause*, supposing blight to be occasioned by insects, instead of attributing the generation of insects to the corruption consequent upon blights, and Bradley makes a voyage to the northeast ' where the cold is intense enough to

give life to those small creatures,' bringing across the seas myriads of them to blight our vegetables ; as if it were not so much easier to manufacture them *logically* at home, than to import them from Nova Zembla A wonderful deal of ingenious conjecture, to be sure, is lost and rendered useless by simply saying, that stagnant fluids, whether vegetable or animal, naturally produce corruption, and that corruption as naturally teems with the seeds of animal life I had once a plant of the Balm of Gilead standing in my window, and by chance it was exposed to a severe northeast wind for several hours, on taking it in, I perceived it to be blighted, the leaves were shrivelled up, the juices became stagnant and extravasated, oozing out in the usual form, from which, no doubt, the insects afterwards observed, were generated, I took the opportunity of looking into this natural process, and found at first the shrivelled leaves contained nothing, but were perfectly dry and parched, in a few hours the liquid, vulgarly called the *honey dew* appeared, and every curled leaf had become a nidus for small green insects, which, in a few days nearly covered the whole plant Now, it was plain to demonstration, that the wind brought neither the *ova* nor the *insects* to the plant, nor aught but corruption to the juices, by its chilling effects It is a common practice in some orchard districts, to make fires on the coming of a blighting wind, which is thought to bring the insects upon its wings, but as it is impossible to counteract or prevent the blast, the fire and smoke might be more efficacious in destroying the eggs or seeds of the insects just on the appearance of the honey-dew Those flies which commit such ravages upon the hop, turnip, and clover, and which have been supposed to come from—no one knows where—most certainly never travelled a hairbreadth from home, where they were generated and hatched The curl in potatoes, about which so much has been said and written, is nothing more nor less than a blight, and to talk about the propagation of it from the seed, is equally rational as to pretend to *propagate the northeast wind* The rigour of the atmospheric stroke or blast of cold wind acting upon the surface of the vegetable body, either entirely dessicates, or dries and withers it, or, suddenly closing the pores and sap vessels, causes an obstruction of the juices whilst the cold continues, but should a milder temperature return gradually, the evil may be self-amended; the obstructed pores will be unlocked by degrees, the regular perspiration of the plant return, and no disease ensue but should the cold stroke be succeeded by sudden heat, or hot gleams of the sun, the obstructed fluids will be at once let loose, and produce those morbid effects so often witnessed; and, exactly on the same principle, if a frosted limb be suddenly exposed to the action of heat, the consequence will be, too rapid a solution of the congealed humours, inflammation, probably gangrene and loss of limb; but placing the limb in a moderate degree of cold, and even rubbing it constantly with cold water, and suffering it to approach the fire by slow degrees, will have an opposite and salutary effect It will be perceived that the ancient doctrine of *catching cold from obstructed perspiration*

—which common sense seems to have rendered impregnable to the modern batteries against it, is adhered to I have known both men and beasts, with constitutions seemingly of adamant, and flesh of so close and hard a texture as to defy all the fair and open attacks of the atmosphere, droop and sink under a stroke of air through a passage, and the maladies of such are usually dangerous, in proportion to the inflammatory powers of their constitution, a single and minute part of the body, such as the corner of an eye or a portion of the jaw, shall be the object of this stroke, in like manner, as a few grains of wheat on one side of an ear shall be affected by the same cause The plague itself is, doubtless, an atmospheric disease, or the consequence of stagnant vapour, and it has been remarked by travellers in the Morea, that during the prevalence of that disease, a blue mist is observable upon the ears of the wheat, which is generally a forerunner of smut, all vegetation still appearing in a most luxuriant and flourishing state

"Every observer will find that the effects of blight depend entirely on the state of the atmosphere for their *continuance* or *recession;* and should they even have advanced to a considerable degree of maturity, warm showers of rain and a continuance of seasonable weather, will prove an effectual remedy; vegetation will regain its natural and healthy colour, the insects will perish, and the mildew and honey-dew disappear—fresh supplies of each will, however, return with the recurrence of the original cause, and such changes often happen in variable seasons, and it is remarkable that insects make their appearance after the access of blight, much sooner upon most, perhaps *all other* vegetables than upon grain

"On the 26th of June, 1804, between seven and eight o'clock in the evening, I was admiring a plot of cauliflowers, which I had planted with a particular experimental view, the plants were of a most luxuriant growth, and the verdure of the leaves most blooming and beautiful, exhibiting in profusion that gloss and those shining tints which are observable on the leaves of grass-proud wheat a warm and genial alteration of the weather, with mild and refreshing southwest breezes had recently prevailed the evening was remarkably warm in an instant, however, one of those rapid changes, for which that inclement season was remarkable, supervened, and I was driven with my companions, by the smartness of a chill which we should not have thought unseasonable at Christmas, into the house, and even to the fireside The sudden decrease of the temperature of that night affected the eyes, throat, and breast of many people, and within a day or two, I had in consequence of the same, several patients on my hands, labouring under symptoms of genuine influenza On the following morning—the 27th—I saw, without surprise, that the leaves of the cauliflower plants were all curled, even the strongest and finest of them, their bloom withered, and their colour become paler by several shades, the weakest plants were most affected by the curl and their leaves became blemished with white specks or spots The wind sat to the northward of the east and the morning was cold, but towards

noon the plants were considerably revived and improved in colour by the warmth of the sun and it was remarked that vegetation improved, or remained stationary, or degenerated, according to the course of the wind The nights of the 27th and 28th were piercing cold, and on the 29th, in the morning, the best of the cauliflowers showed a fresh curl upon the leaf, whilst upon the weakly plants which had not recovered from the first shock, the white spots had degenerated into morbid blotches, analogous to those upon the animal body—the consequence of obstructed and vitiated juices The blue mould now made its appearance in the hearts and on the lower leaves, which wore a shrivelled and withered appearance, and in two or three days this mould became animated, in the form of those lice which are proper to the cabbage in its morbid state several of these plants were recovered by the experiment of washing off the mould with water and a brush, and the strongest had nearly recovered their former strength and vigour, when another cold night, with the wind at northeast, succeeding a warm day, prostrated them again"

Frank And now, how plain all this appears—surely there cannot be a question any longer on the subject. But speaking of the obstruction of the sap, reminds me of the promise which you once made me to describe the more modern theory of the *circulation* of the sap: formerly it was supposed merely to *rise and fall*, you know.

Father Yes. I remember having said in one of our former conversations, that when you were older

20*

you must examine and study this theory, and as that time has now arrived, I will endeavour to make you acquainted with an outline of this very singular and interesting process of nature. I once saw a piece of oak placed under a powerful microscope, and had the opportunity of observing the sap passing upwards by one set of vessels, and returning downwards by another set at the same time, thus performing the most perfect *circulation* imaginable. It is supposed that the chief part of the sap ascends by the *albur num*, or soft wood, which is observable in every tree, answering to the name, *sap of timber*, which surrounds the more solid portion of the tree, denominated *the heart of the timber*, and that it descends by the vessels of the bark, or what is called the *liber*, and it would seem too that this theory is just. In a living plant or tree, then, the sap passes up by the inside vessels, and returns downwards by those of the bark, or perhaps between the bark and the albur num, and it is found that, to throw a barren tree into bearing, it is only necessary to cut a narrow ring of bark from the branches to prevent the sap from returning, and it will then be thrown into them, and thus the desired end will be obtained. I was passing a day with a friend some time since, and he showed me a plum tree in his garden which he had reared from seed, but which had never before borne a single fruit it had then a branch loaded with fruit, whilst all the other parts of the tree were barren. He told me his wife had, in the spring, observed a caterpillar's nest immediately on the under side of this branch, and wishing to destroy it, she tied a rag dipped in sulphur

to a long rod, and setting it on fire, held it close to the limb, determined to make sure destruction. In a little time the bark separated from the tree in that part, and showed that it had been completely destroyed by the operation. but when the tree put forth, a great profusion of blossoms appeared, and an abundance of fruit followed. this I saw, and observed that a large piece of the bark had been removed from the under side of the limb, showing signs of fire. Here, the downward passage of the sap had been arrested, and had been thrown into the branch by the destruction of the bark, according to the theory above described, but this had been effected by fire. On remarking this to a person who had a fine garden, he told me he remembered having seen a tree in an adjoining lot that had never borne, but a fire occurring on the adjoining premises, one side of this tree was so scorched that the bark was totally destroyed to a considerable height, when, the next spring, the tree blossomed and bore a profusion of fruit

DIALOGUE XIX

INFLUENCE OF THE FEMALE CHARACTER, POETRY, AND MUSIC

Frank. Father, have you seen the beautiful rose which has just opened in sister Susan's garden? It is indeed splendid. I don't know how it is, but I am no match for Susan in gardening, she has the knack of making every thing flourish which she cultivates, and I have often observed, that if we are planting the cuttings of flowering shrubs, and although I might have dug the land and prepared the cuttings for her, there is not one in five of hers that will die, while out of mine, it is only about one in five that will live   I begin to think there must be some truth in the old-fashioned notion, that when a man is formed, a woman is formed also, the finest portion of the clay being selected for this purpose   All that Susan does, is done with her fingers, whereas all mine seems done by the *rule of thumb !*

Father   There is certainly a difference in the way in which you and Susan do things, but I am by no means inclined to make the comparison to your disadvantage   I confess there is much beauty in that old-fashioned idea which you have mentioned , and with us, who know and taste and feel the value of the female character, it is no wonder that it should have some weight   but *we* are fortunate in this respect, remember

Frank   I declare, I fancy that I perceive a difference in the fragrance of sister Susan's flowers when compared with mine, and certainly they continue longer in bloom

Father   That I dare say is only a fancy, yet it is a pleasing one, to which I suppose, you have not much objection   The idea, that to the finer mould of the female is to be attributed the power, which they assuredly possess, of bearing with more fortitude the reverses of fortune, and the bereavements of life than men, is beautiful and quite poetical ; and many are the instances which I have known, where, after sus-

taining her full share of the trouble and anguish consequent upon such, the wife has been able to impart a portion of her mental courage to the support of a husband, bowed to the earth with the weight of his share of affliction   Like a china cup, into which boiling water might be poured, and, immediately after, water cold as ice, without fear of breaking—so the heart of woman will expand with prosperity and contract with adversity, without bursting , while the man, like a brown-ware mug, is done up in half the time !

Frank   Well, I never heard any one advocate so well the cause of woman in my life !

Father   Ah ha ! that reminds me of an occurrence which took place some years ago, and which I must relate to you   I was travelling by coach in England in company with six gentlemen, and a plain homely woman about sixty years of age   the subject of conversation amongst the men was, the character of the female sex , and although they agreed, that the women were the *weaker* sex, they dissented in toto to the doctrine of their being the *softer*   I, as I always do, vindicated their *rights and privileges* , and on my remarking that they were formed of the finer clay, the old lady, who had long felt intense interest in the conversation, exclaimed   " well ! indeed I never heard any one talk so well in my life !   I declare it quite does me good to hear you, sir !"   About the same time, I crossed the channel between Ryde and Portsmouth in a sailing boat, on a stormy day   the passengers had taken their seats, when a very elegant young man, in the military dress of a foreigner, came on board, and inquired in broken English, if any lady wanted a protector for the passage? The *ladies,* all but one old fishwoman with a basket of fish for the Portsmouth market, had already been suited with partners, and she, being the only unprotected female, he went and took his seat beside her, pulled her cloak about her head and feet, and waited upon her with the greatest assiduity The old woman did not at first know what to make of it, but after a little, she winked to the rest of the passengers, and quite enjoyed it The gentleman, seeing them smile, said "Gentlemen, I am a Knight of the Prussian Order of the *North Star*, our only bond of union is the protection of woman, at all times and in all places, without regard to age or beauty" On our arrival at Portsmouth, he offered the old woman his arm, took the basket of fish in the other hand, and stepped gracefully on shore, handed her the fish, made her a bow, and walked on The old woman could contain no longer, but bursting into a scream of laughter, declared it was the *rummest* joke that she had ever seen or heard of

I grant that it is not in your power to imitate your sister in the delicate and gentle way in which she nurses her tender charge—raising their drooping heads, looking them in the face, and calling them "my pretties," for *she,* I am sure you will admit, *is* one of the softer sex And this reminds me of that beautiful poetic gem, "The Hymn to the Flowers," by Horace Smith, which was republished in the Farmers' Cabinet a few months ago, the endearing epithets with which many of the verses commence,

are particularly delicate and affecting, and although I have read and repeated it times innumerable, I still experience new delight on every fresh perusal You must copy it into your book, and get it by heart, and then you will never be at a loss for a beautiful simile at sight of a beautiful and lovely flower

Frank Shall I read it?

Father Do so, and *study it*, without which one half its beauties are undiscernible it is the finest lesson in poetry that I know

HYMN TO THE FLOWERS

Day-stars' that ope your eyes with man, to twinkle,
  From rainbow galaxies of earth's creation,
And dew drops on her lonely altars sprinkle,
    As a libation—

Ye matin worshippers' who, bending lowly,
  Before th' uprisen sun, God's lidless eye,
Throw from your chalices a sweet and holy
    Incense on high'

Ye bright Mosaics' that with storied beauty,
  The floor of Nature's temple tesselate,
What num'rous emblems of instructive duty,
    Your forms create'

'Neath clustered boughs, each floral bell that swingeth,
  And tolls its perfume on the passing air,
Makes Sabbath in the fields, and ever ringeth,
    A call to prayer'

Not to the domes, where crumbling arch and column,
  Attest the feebleness of mortal hand,
But to that fane, most catholic and solemn,
    Which God hath plann'd—

To that cathedral, boundless as our wonder,
   Whose quenchless lamps the sun and moon supply,
Its choir the winds and waves—its organ thunder—
     Its dome the sky'

There, as in solitude and shade I wander,
   Through the green aisles, or stretched upon the sod,
Awed by the silence, reverently ponder
     The ways of God—

Your voiceless lips, O flowers, are living preachers,
   Each cup a pulpit, every leaf a book,
Supplying to my fancy numerous teachers,
     From loneliest nook

Floral apostles! that in dewy splendour,
   "Weep without wo, and blush without a crime,"
Oh' may I deeply learn and ne'er surrender
     Your lore sublime'

"Thou wert not, Solomon, in all thy glory,
   Arrayed," the lilies cry, "in robes like ours,
How vain your grandeur'—ah' how transitory
     Are *human* flowers'"

In the sweet-scented pictures, Heavenly Artist'
   With which thou paintest nature's wide-spread hall,
What a delightful lesson thou impartest,
     Of love to all'

Not useless are ye, flowers, though made for pleasure,
   Blooming o'er field and wave, by day and night,
From every source your sanction bids me treasure
     Harmless delight'

Ephemeral sages' what instructors hoary,
   For such a world of thought could furnish scope'
Each fading calyx a *memento mori,*
     Yet fount of hope'

Posthumous glories' angel-like collection,
   Upraised from seed or bulb interred in earth,
Ye are to me a type of resurrection,
     And second birth'

Were I, O God' in churchless lands remaining,
   Far from all voice of teachers and divines,
My soul would find, in flowers of thy ordaining,
     Priests, sermons, shrines'

Frank Well, that is the most beautiful piece of poetry I ever read' I long to read it to Susan, how well she will understand it, and how much she will admire it' It is a *gem,* indeed

Father Its re-publication in the Farmers' Cabinet, called forth an article, in the succeeding number, from the pen of a practical farmer, and as it bears so immediately on the subject of our present conversation, I wish you to copy it, you will, I think, find it interesting and instructive It begins thus—

To the Editor of the Farmers' Cabinet.

Sir—On returning from my day's task, that of turning an acre of land with one of " Prouty's long sods," I found my wife and daughters busily engaged in *turning over* the pages of the May number of the Cabinet, in the hope of finding more poetry like that exquisite " Hymn to the Flowers," at page 285 If, Mr Editor, you continue to interest the female portion of our families, your business is done, no one can calculate the influence of the women, and when that is in a right direction, every thing goes well

I never visit a family for the first time, without

examining very closely the characters of the females belonging to it, if these are intelligent, and fond of reading and poetry, I know that all is right, and if the daughters keep a *scrap-book*, I am sure that every thing in the house and around the house is as it should be indeed the influence of the scrap-book may be traced even to the garden, for what girl who is fond of flowers and poetry, will allow her parterre to be overgrown with weeds? And then the next thing is, to witness the honeysuckles twining around the door, and creeping in at the windows! When I was a young man in search of a wife, I always considered such prognostics a sure *sign* that *good entertainment* was to be found within, and the choice which I was so fortunate as to make from such a recommendation, emboldens me to press it upon the notice of all who are upon the same errand

But to return to that gem, "The Hymn to the Flowers" You must know, sir, that the law in our family is, to have as little as possible to do on a Sunday, that it may be, indeed, a "Sabbath," a day of rest to man and beast To this end, my wife and daughters vie with each other in preparing for it on the Saturday, all that can then be done *is* done, even to the decoration of the parlour with fresh flowers after a thorough cleaning and righting, so that when we rise on the Sunday-morning—which we always do earlier than on any other day—we feel the luxury of a "Sabbath morning"

My house is situated within a short distance of the church, and after an early breakfast, and while the

women are putting things away, and preparing for their approaching duties, (my daughters are teachers in the Sabbath-school,) it is my custom to visit all the animals upon the farm, to congratulate them upon the return of their day of rest—their holiday—and then to enter the wood which adjoins the garden, throw myself upon the sod, and repeat, from beginning to end, "The Hymn to the Flowers," applying those endearing epithets with which the verses commence, to them in person—

Floral apostles' that in dewy splendour
"Weep without wo, and blush without a crime'"
Oh' may I deeply learn and ne'er surrender
Your lore sublime'

But it is not possible for me to describe my feelings, or the devotion which springs up within me on such occasions—they are the holiest of the holy, and attune my heart to the performance of the church, in a way quite unutterable! Need I say, that after such a "Sabbath of the soul," we begin the week with an elasticity of feeling which gives such an impetus to our exertions, as carries us clean through till Saturday night!

My daughters request me to hand you, in return for the pleasure which they have experienced in the perusal of the above hymn, an extract from their *scrap-book*, which they hope will be deemed worthy your acceptance, it is from Moore's selection of "Irish Melodies," and is, perhaps, one of the most *melodious*—

Oh' had we some bright little isle of our own,
In a blue summer ocean, far off, and alone,
Where a leaf never dies in the still blooming bowers,
And the bee banquets on through a whole year of flowers—
     Where the sun loves to pause
     With so fond a delay,
     That the night only draws
     A thin veil o'er the day—
Where, simply to feel that we breathe—that we live—
Is worth the best joy that life elsewhere can give

There, with souls ever ardent, and pure as the clime,
We should love as *they* loved in the first golden time'
The glow of the sunshine, the balm of the air,
Would steal to our hearts, and make all summer there
     With affection as free
     From decline as the bowers,
     And with hope, like the bee,
     Living always on flowers,
Our lives would resemble a long day of light,
And our death come on holy and calm as the night'

Frank Well, that is a heavenly melody! But, father, have you not noticed that, meet Farmer Sykes when we will, he is always singing? I never heard neighbour Grabb sing or whistle I think their *clay* must have been different at the first, and while one might be likened to the *happy soil*, the other must have been, what is the horror of all good farmers, a *weepy soil*

Father Ay, Sykes has a soul to feel, as well as a tongue to express by heavenly sounds the language of the heart I am sure that his love of sacred music might be traced in all that he does—in his ploughing,

in his sowing, in his weeding, and in his mowing, and especially in the management of his cattle and horses, to whom he *chants* his commands, instead of uttering them in that brutal tone and expression in general use amongst farmers And when we hear the observation, " The farmer's eye makes the horse fat," I cannot but think, " the farmer's tongue" does quite as much in that friendly office And you must often have observed, when Sykes unties his horses in the stable for the purpose of harnessing them for their labour, and says, " Come, my beauties," how quickly they turn in their stalls, and stretch out their necks, and open their mouths to receive the bit, and I have seen his saddle-horse carry the whip in his mouth, and gallop with his master on his back'

Frank All this is true, but you have been all this while drawing your own, as well as Farmer Sykes's portrait, you know

Father No one would calculate the advantages arising from a mild and gentle spirit wherever cattle, sheep and other animals are kept, but this we might see exemplified in the conduct of those around us, for we know that Farmer Blunden's two dogs and his two more savage sons are the terror of the neighbourhood, while his poor animals are worried almost to death by incessant noise and driving His dairy is ruined by such means, for his cows are brought up to be milked on the gallop, and their return to pasture is a perfect *cow-hunt'* while the bloody ears of his sheep and hogs show that the hunters are often *in at the death* Now, they complain that their milk will not keep, and it is notorious that they make